Charles A. Stephens

Pluri-Cellular Man

Whence and what is the intellect

Charles A. Stephens

Pluri-Cellular Man
Whence and what is the intellect

ISBN/EAN: 9783337314385

Printed in Europe, USA, Canada, Australia, Japan

Cover: Foto ©Thomas Meinert / pixelio.de

More available books at **www.hansebooks.com**

PLURI-CELLULAR MAN.

WHENCE AND WHAT IS THE INTELLECT, OR "SOUL"?

WHAT BECOMES OF THE SOUL?

IS IT POSSIBLE TO SAVE THE SOUL?

FROM

THE BIOLOGICAL STANDPOINT.

BY

C. A. STEPHENS, A. M., M. D.

THE LABORATORY COMPANY,

NORWAY LAKE, MAINE.

1892.

CONTENTS.

INTRODUCTORY NOTE.

In a small volume published in 1888, the author set forth the Sentient Hypothesis of matter at considerable length, from which the following paragraphs may be here quoted : —

" We conceive of matter as sentient, and that its sentience is a constant, constantly expended in motion and every form of dynamic energy, and as constantly renewed in the cycle of the universe. Sentience is the origin and end of all natural phenomena. Matter moves and returns to itself through the great cycle of universal phenomena. Matter possesses the elements of *feeling;* hence the universe has everywhere a low degree of sense, — *sense* to proceed toward an object ; and this sense to proceed toward an object 'is that which gives semblance of design in nature.

" Gravitation and natural phenomena result from the primary sentient impulse : a static impulse which constitutes matter what we behold it to be.

" What seems the inertia of matter is a condition of equilibration; what appears to be dead matter is only matter at a deadlock, from which it may be released to live. This *living*, that is to say, primarily sentient, property is eternal to and inseparable from the ultimate atom, a *constant* amid the changing phenomena of sun and world systems; and even when locked in the apparently dead clod, or stick, or stone, the initial atoms are still living atoms, robbed of not one whit of their static ability to feel and to live. Such is the present conception.

" Philosophy taught much concerning certain supposititious properties of matter, and has portrayed its impenetrability, porosity, extensibility, ductility, inertia, *et al.* These were held to be its prime properties. As a necessity of theological tenets, matter was depicted as the lifeless material of a manufactured universe.

" But the philosophy of to-day postulates matter, not as life-less but as living; not the inert substance of a created world, but the living substance of a self-creating and self-sustaining universe; that matter is itself *creative* of natural phenomena by virtue of that static attribute which resides at the core of every atom.

" Atomicity, however, is a depth of matter of which we yet know little; the *life* of unorganized matter is expressed mainly in the effects which we term gravitation and the natural forces. Of atoms such as probably radiate from the sun, no apparatus yet devised by man enables us to obtain definition in terms of weight or size.

" We know that we stand upon something solid and resistant to touch. This is the testimony of sense. Whether the atoms be ' physical points,' centres of radiation of energy, is as debatable to-day as in Berkeley's time. Nor is it likely that a solution of this problem can be immediately reached, since all our knowledge points to a well-nigh infinite subdivision and rarefaction of matter. But, as an incident of the broadening of knowledge in this particular, there may be remarked the return of scientific opinion from the extremes of the dynamic hypothesis toward the Newtonian doctrine of matter. To treat of *force* as something distinct from matter is a solecism.

" That the sentient theory does, in very truth, found on a lower basis of fact and discloses a law of phenomena not hitherto set forth in any scheme of nature, no one who will observe its application to physical and vital problems, thus far obscure, can long doubt. It portrays a universe, acting of itself, without interference. It presents as ' unknowable,' or as yet unknown, but one thing — *matter*. The sentient or vital hypothesis of the universe assumes, primarily, that matter, the basis substance of sensible nature, is creative of the universe by virtue of a single primary property — sentience.

" The philosophic argument for this hypothesis is the same given for every doctrine of either matter or deity, since men first reasoned ; namely, its simplicity, consisting in (1) the fact that it accounts more fully for all phenomena than any other hypothesis ; and (2) that it accounts for such phenomena with the assumption of fewest unknown quantities. And herein lies all the *a priori* proof that has ever been advanced for any world hypothesis, or that ever can be advanced in evidence. We reason, and can reason on no other basis.

" The sentient particles *feel*, and from this eternal well-spring all phenomena, physical and vital, move forth. Rather there are no physical phenomena in the sense of an insentient force. All motion originates from the elementary sentience. Hence, in organized matter, we contemplate, not the miracle of an insentient force transforming itself into sentience and intelligence, but simply the raising-up of this primary sentience of matter to more full expression. The organism of any living creature is the instrument developed and employed by the inherent sentience of its component particles to obtain wider, fuller feeling.

" The moral effect of this later conception of matter and of nature is strong and far-reaching.

" It means kinship and brotherhood with all nature about us. It means love and sympathy, not only for all living things, but for earth, air, and sky, for the great sentient environment out of which we have emerged, and a part of which we are. For it is when we are in such sympathy and co-relation with the universe around us that we live in fullest measure. Alienation is death. We die as we grow callous to the world around us, and that is a false creed which instructs to forgetfulness of earth and a direction of the heart and mind to a foreign state of existence. Such alienation is a hastening on to the apathy of old age. We are to be taught to live, not to die. It is a most hopeful fact that all the enormous falsehood which forms the burden and the shame of literature, namely, that earth is a dreary place and life a miserable bourn, has never really alienated the great warm heart of humanity from this dear old earth, the birthplace and home of all the human generations."

This doctrine of matter (by no means new, since it was the doctrine of Gassendi in 1640, of Tyndall in 1870 ; and in the classic era, of Epikuros, Demokritos and Lucretius) was variously and unfavorably criticised in 1889, as a " recent form of scientific materialism." It is not without gratification, therefore, that after three

years the author finds his views indorsed and assented
to by practical investigators like Thomas Edison, Dr.
Hyslop, Dr. Wm. Thompson and Prof. Sterry Hunt.

In November, 1891, Mr. Edison says : —

" It is my belief that every atom of matter is *intelligent*, deriv-
ing energy from the primordial germ.   The intelligence of man
is, I take it, the sum of the intelligences of the atoms of which
he is composed.   Every atom has an intelligent power of selec-
tion and is always striving to get into harmonious relation with
other atoms. . . . All matter lives and everything that lives
possesses intelligence. . . . The atom is conscious if man is
conscious, is intelligent if man is intelligent, exercises will power
if man does.

" We are told by geologists that in the earliest periods no form
of life could exist on the earth.   How do they know that ?   A
crystal is devoid of this vital principle they say, and yet certain
kinds of atoms invariably arrange themselves in a particular
way to form a crystal.   They did that in geological periods,
antedating the appearance of any form of life, and have been
doing it ever since, in precisely the same way.   Some crystals
form in branches like a fern.   Why is there not life in the
growth of a crystal ?   Was the vital principle specially created
at some particular period of the earth's history, or did it exist
and control every atom of matter when the earth was molten ?
I cannot avoid the conclusion that all matter is composed of
intelligent atoms, and that life and mind are merely synonymes
for the aggregation of atomic intelligence."

The half-dozen papers, which form the present
volume, are incidental to an extended investigation of
the causes of "old age" and organic death, with a
view to the prolongation of human life; — incidental
and explanatory rather than strictly pertinent to it.
The motive in publishing them and others which will
follow, is a desire to make plain the *data* and purposes
of the investigation.   At first thought, the effort to
prolong healthy individual life, by the practical appli-

cation of recent discoveries in biological science, would seem to require neither vindication nor apology. If the life of a normal useful human being can be prolonged to a century, a century and a half, or even indefinitely, why not? None the less, many grave social and ethical questions are thought to be involved in such a proposition; and it appears necessary to clear the way, so to speak, for the reception of the proposition, even among the well-educated.

I find it also expedient to add, in view of many inquiries made, that the prolongation of life sought from this investigation is not expected to come from "elixirs," nor any of those picturesque -osophies and -ologies which periodically enlist the enthusiasm of many susceptible persons; but rather on those well-defined lines of human evolution along which man has risen from his anthropoid ancestry, and already prolonged his life-time from fifteen and twenty years to seventy-five and a hundred; the point especially in view at present being that these long-operative lines and agencies of human progress may be taken under intelligent control and immensely facilitated by the application of recent science.

PLURICELLULAR MAN.

I.

LIVING MATTER.

ACCORDING to as good an estimate as can be made at present, — taking into account not alone animals and plants, but germs and infusorial orders of life, in the water, air and superficies of the soil, — there is in the living condition (protoplasm) a quantity of matter which would equal a stratum at least one centimeter in thickness, over land and sea; or over an area of 197,120,000 square miles.

In other words, there is existent on the earth 177,-346,336,000,000 cubic feet of living matter, or protoplasm. By this we mean to convey the idea that such a part of the terrestrial globe is constantly in the living condition, similarly as another portion is in the aqueous condition, or as still another is in the aerial, or the argillaceous, or the carbonaceous condition. It is matter quite the same, in fact, identical, in many cases, and may readily pass from the living to the non-living condition and *vice versa*.

This mass of living matter weighs 5,500,460,500,000 tons: sufficient weight and bulk to make a small planet of itself.

It is ordinary matter, *i. e.*, oxygen, hydrogen, nitrogen, carbon, sulphur, phosphorus, etc., differing, so far as the closest examination which we can give it shows, in no respect from these same, so-called, "elements" in other situations and combinations of non-living matter; nor is there reason for believing, that, while in the living condition, it really possesses essentially different properties, or powers than when in the non-living condition. It is simply, so far as can be learned, that when in the living condition, the *arrangement of the particles is different;* and from this difference of arrangement and grouping, a common property, or *constant,* of matter finds scope for action in a new and different manner which we term *life.*

Kepler as is known entertained a vagrant opinion that the earth is a living creature possessing *nous,* also lungs; subject to ailments, a vast *amœba,* swimming in the ethereal seas of space.

The more practical science of this century smiles at the foible of the studious old Wirtemburger; and yet it can be asserted in strictest truth that a very considerable portion of the earth is alive.

In the broad sense, regarding the earth as we should regard it if observing it from some outer point in space, the standpoint of one of the earth's companion planets, for example, we may represent this living part of the earth as a cortex, or stratum, one of its outer strata, enclosing it over its entire surface.

A significant almost startling phase of it is, that this vast quantity of matter is constantly passing out of the living into the non-living condition. As often as once in six hours, probably, once in twelve certainly on an average, the entire five or six trillions of tons of protoplasmic matter falls out of the living into the non-living condition; and *pari passu* an equally vast

weight of non-living matter is raised up into protoplasm. It is believed that all or the most part of the
matter which makes up the outer strata of the earth to
the depth of many miles, has at some time or other
been in the living state, and not once or twice only but
many times — a million times very likely.

We may, indeed, go much farther and not exceed
what is probable in supposing that in the great past
history of the universe — a history of successive series
of solar and planetary formations — matter has lived in
an infinite number of forms and types of life from eternity, intermittently and alternately.

The power which facilitates the passage of this enormous body of matter into the living condition and sustains it there, consists largely in those dynamic effects
which come from outer, grander bodies of matter, more
especially the sun, — stimulus in the form of an ethereal
influx of matter in extreme tenuity, set in swift movement by vast mutations of matter afar.

For here it is significant to note the reversion of
scientific opinion from the extremes of the dynamic
hypothesis of *pure* force toward the Newtonian idea.
Light and also heat and electricity are not only dynamic,
but material. Force, so far as we know of it, is always
associated with an efflux of matter.

The method by which this continuous passage of non-
living into living matter is effected, is association and
contact with previously existing living matter. The
non-living must be infused into the living matter ere the
non-living can be re-vitalized.

The intimate impulse which accomplishes this vast
transfiguration is *subjective*, resident in the protoplasm
itself, or in other words, in the matter which is, for the

passing hour, in the living condition, and which sinks
down from that living condition, while in the act of
raising up non-living matter to its own level.   The
impulse, or working energy, is apparently a transgres-
sion of subjective sentience into matter-moving power
or motion, effected at a great depth of atomicity on that
low plane where particles are able to move in response
to a primarily sentient property which they universally
possess.

It is from this low plane or condition of tenuity, that
protoplasm is built up, and sets forth in its wonderful
career, bearing feeling, intelligence, and mind outward
among inert, coarser masses of matter.   For the earth's
superficies, it must always be borne in mind, is a hard
theatre for life.   On the earth as we find it and now
inhabit it, life struggles upward from this deep-lying,
vital plane of matter in the teeth of a gigantic resistance.   The energy in protoplasm is largely expended
in overcoming this molar resistance ; the bulk of our
living substance has necessarily been impressed into
mechanical service, — bone, teeth, hair, cuticle, muscle,
tendon, in order to make way and obtain food.   This,
in fact, is life on earth, as man has thus far led it ;
but it is possible to improve the earth as a theatre of
life, and by the control and regulation of its "natural
forces" to lessen the resistance.   This, indeed, has been
one of the aspirations and religious dreams of humanity during all historic time—"Heaven"—and this,
I suppose, will be the realization of the dream, namely,
the paradisation of earth.   Even during our own generation the domination of the electric and magnetic
forces of matter will be a long step in that direction.
Man may win his longed-for heaven at last ; and it
will not be a gift to him, but an achievement.

As yet we know no method of transmuting non-living into living matter apart from the agency of previously existent living matter. No more can we transmute carbon into diamond, even when we have existent diamonds present; nor yet can we make feldspar, or mica, or gold, or silver, or lead. It is as likely that we shall discover a method of producing living matter, as that we shall learn to produce any of these substances.

It is quite possible that living matter still continues to come into existence on the earth's surface under certain circumstances; probable also that at a former period of the earth's history, the conditions, thermal and electro-magnetic, may have been much more favorable to the passage of matter into the living state than at present; for certain it is, that there have been epochs during which a far vaster quantity of matter was continuously in the living condition than at present.

If a telluric catastrophe, attended by the production of great heat or mephitic gases, were to kill, or reduce this great stratum of living matter to the non-living condition, the earth, at the present climacteric of its existence as a life-producing globe, might, hereafter, lie fallow and lifeless. It seems more probable, however, that protoplasm (micro-organisms) would again be renewed upon it in lowly form, and that another slow cycle of vital evolution would begin, although under less favorable conditions than in earlier ages. That pluricellular organisms would develop, is somewhat doubtful.

A uniform temperature of 100° Centigrade, continued for a few hours, would suffice to terminate the present terrestrial life era; yet in the cooling process, amidst the lukewarm masses of lifeless proteid matter, new particles might fortuitously be lifted to the living condition, and the grand struggle to live again be inaugurated.

It has been argued, on the other hand, that the earth could never have produced protoplasm originally; that it is impossible, under any conceivable terrestrial conditions, that particles of non-living matter should have been lifted into the composite, complex arrangement of the protoplasmic molecule; and that the earliest *protozoa*, or their spores, must have come to the earth in meteoric or cosmic matter, hailing from some world in space where other physical conditions prevail, more favorable to life; in a word, that life is not indigenous on the earth but immigrant and of alien birth. But we are more inclined to believe, with the ancient sages, that the earth is truly our common Mother.

The point made or mooted by the "alien" hypotheses is, that from the tension of the natural forces in the terrestrial mass and the physical resistance to vital action protoplasm could never have come into existence spontaneously; also, that having by chance or intelligent design been transplanted into terrestrial matter, the struggle to live is one against nature, the nature of the environment. In a word, that we are "pilgrims and strangers" on the earth, sighing for another world. This conception has found utterance in the grim doctrines of "Mother Ann" and the Shakers, and in the philosophical writings of Schopenhauer *et al.*

But there is no good nor sufficient evidence that life is alien or unnatural. Rather the reverse. The probabilities are a hundred to one, that protoplasm originated on the earth and that life is native,

None the less, there are certain indications that the earth has reached, or passed, its life-originating period; that it will never again be parturient of new types and genera, although for millions of years it may remain a temperate *habitat* for its children already born and grown; and that some of those grown to adult estate may yet acquire well-nigh divine powers and achieve that dream of the ages, — immunity from disease and death.

One reason for believing that new protoplasm and new protozoa no longer come into existence spontaneously, is that many or all of the micro-organisms which we study under the microscope are new only in the sense of being newly discovered by us. The disease-bacteria were at least operative and produced the same ptomaines three thousand years ago. The Diatomaceæ of to-day exhibit the same characteristics and the same silicious envelope as those taken from fossiliferous strata laid down in the seas of the Carboniferous period. In fact, many of the genera of micro-organisms are the most venerable and changeless of any upon the earth. Nor can we wholly agree with those who regard these minute creatures as the most rudimentary of living forms. It by no means follows that because a living creature is small, that it is hence exceedingly simple and recent in the sense of ancestry and heredity.

Another feature of this vast body of terrestrial living matter, the most remarkable and important feature indeed, is the singular mode in which it exists or lives, from moment to moment. Although of such vast bulk and weight when considered in the aggregate, it is never found in continuous bulk, but always exists as minute *modica*, or little measures, isolated one from another, scattered throughout and embedded in non-living matter. On an average, these minute *modica* of living matter or protoprasm are not much more than the three-thousandth of an inch in diameter, but occasionally reach the one two-hundredth ; and their true or typical form is manifestly spheroidal. From the centre of these small spnerules, life is exhibited as a series of attractions and repulsions, exerted upon particles of non-living matter. In consistency, the living substance is semi-fluid ; it is so nearly transparent as to be deemed color-less ; and it does not give off odorous particles. As above remarked, it is ordinary matter, oxygen, hydro-gen, nitrogen, carbon, etc., and the cause of its peculiar behavior, in the living condition, is in all probability the manner in which the particles are combined, and their arrangement and relations one with another.

More profoundly, when we seek to know why living matter assumes the form of and exists always in the small spherical integers, termed " cells," we are brought to the investigation of a new law of matter which ap-parently acts counter to gravitation, or, as is more likely, prevails upon an interior plane of matter within that on which gravitation acts. It is the sway and prev-alence of gravitation over ordinary matter which causes the world of matter, as we see it, to appear lifeless and inert. But in protoplasm, pure and un-alloyed, we behold a law of matter find expression subversive of gravity, prevalent over it and transfigur-ing ordinary matter to living matter in spite of gravity, so to speak. This may seem a bold statement. Life, indeed, has been held by many biologists to be a co-relative of gravitation, a cognate and derivative mode of the universal energy of matter. Cognate, indeed, it no doubt is; derivative also in the loose sense of being aided and facilitated by it in all the larger forms of terrestrial life; for it is assuredly not the intention here to convey the idea that the ordinary functions of animals are carried on contrary to gravity, or chemism. The writer ventures, however, to set forth the conception that within a normal "cell" of living matter there is an expression of energy not derived from general gravitation, but superior to it; as if emanating from an inner seat of energy, as if acting upon matter at a different angle or *point d'appui.* Such an opinion by no means conflicts with the monistic conception of energy. It is meant merely to set forth that life is not the immediate derivative of gravitation, or chemism, which many physical philosophers have been inclined to consider it, but rather a static property of matter which antedates gravity, and, in the intimate composition of matter, outranks it.

Indeed, the truer view of this great question is probably that *life* finds but an irregular, erratic expression in the superficies of the terrestrial globe, where gravity and the more gross modes of universal energy prevail as a rule. Yet the conception will be found to grow in the mind of the student of living matter, that this wonderful static property is a very universal property; in a word, that all matter is *sentient* at bottom; and that its apparent *insentience* or lifelessness and inertia, as seen on the earth, is less a natural than an unnatural and fortuitous condition into which it has fallen from the peculiar recoils incident to planetary formation.

This view need not incline the student to entertain pantheistic conceptions of matter, or drift away to extreme opinions as to a universal mind in nature, —

an ocean of omniscient intellect, from which our
" souls " are stray driblets.   On the contrary, the entire trend and drift of biological science are to the
effect that the primary static property of matter is
sentience only in the sense that the raw flax is dam-
ask ; that the crude ore is a steel cruiser, and that in
the great tracts of universal matter, there is nothing
more intelligent than the *possibility of intelligence* as
a result and fruit of a vast cycle of protoplasmic evolution ; even as in protoplasm of lowly grade there is
little save the capacity to feel. Be it remembered, too,
that there is now, probably, no protoplasm existent on
the earth's surface of such lowly grade, such archaic
simplicity upon the scale of intelligence, as that which
first stirred on the early shores of the azoic oceans.

Indeed, it seems to me that the untaught human
blunder of deifying the great unintelligent, material
energy of nature has led to much mischief in all our
religious concepts.   It is better, morally, to regard
nature as but rudimentarily intelligent, and the human
intellect as the highest fruit of nature's long effort to
live and grow in knowledge.

As the student examines those wonderful little integers, the " cells," day by day, the inquiry constantly
presents itself, Why does the living matter adopt this
form?   Why does it live in these little globules of
uniform size? — for although the size of cells differs
considerably relatively to each other in different tissues
and situations, the difference is mainly within certain
definite limits ; and the general type and form are
unmistakable and apparently unchangeable.

Why does protoplasm exist in such small measures
of substance, each scarcely more than a pin's point?

Why do its " cells " fail, since they are constantly growing, to attain larger size, an inch or more in diameter?
Why do they not coalesce in the tissues into one sentient
working mass? And why, on the contrary, do they
constantly divide, when these small dimensions are
reached, and become dormant, die even, rather than
transgress them? These are inquiries which the student will find often recurring as he observes cell life.
The idea conveyed from the totality of such question-
ings, is one of a certain ever-present barrier to protoplasmic life, or a constantly restricting law.

As regards the larger pluricellular organisms, however, the immediate answer is not far to seek. For all
these — the metazoans, man, and other mammals, for
example — are pluricellular creatures in the sense not
only of being composed of many cells, but also of having a derivative origin from unicellular life. The
earlier metazoans were banded protozoans, loosely
confederated groups of unicellular creatures, which for
a period of their existence remained in a kind of union
and afterwards disbanded to go their individual, unicellular ways.

There is reason to believe that the arrangement of
matter in protoplasm, as we find it in different animals
and plants, is very complex. For example, the protoplasm in an oak certainly differs much from that in a
pine, and that of both much from that in a man : differences well exhibited by the diversity of the substances
which result from their growth. These differences can be
eradicated in no perceptible degree by any processes of
nurture which we are able to apply to the protoplasm
in periods of time which human science has knowledge
of, and they are believed to have resulted from a slow

process of development in accord with certain long-standing telluric conditions, through epochs of time which must be measured by millions of years.

It cannot be otherwise than that this tiny dot of transparent semi-fluid matter in the cell of the oak sap-wood, or of the human brain, small as it looks to be, is yet the repository of effects which have accumulated and been stored in it through all this vast time period. Nor is the concept difficult to grasp. For were this protoplasmic dot magnified till it assumed before our eyes the size of a planet, the ultimate atom-particles of matter would still remain invisible to human sight. There is, therefore, material scope and room, so to speak, in the protoplasmic " cell " for differential growth and generic evolution for all time. In the dot of pro-toplasm, visible only under high microscopic powers, are undoubtedly material particles in such numbers that no system of arithmetical notation known to us could enumerate them. Something of this we know from computations of light waves; *i. e.*, we know that the " atom " must be not *more* than a sextillionth of an inch in diameter. But how much *less* may it be? This " atom " may be a solar orb down there.

It is well to practise the mind in such thought, for one of the stumbling blocks of our time is lack of faith in nature. He who permanently fills his mind with good relative ideas of the known immensity and capacity of matter, will not find himself barren of hope or delin-quent in faith in nature and his race. It helps us to get away from that old night-mare of Semitic dogma, which for centuries has misrepresented the earth as " originally cursed," and humanity as " damned."

If there is an aspect of nature more manifest than

another, it is the aspect of vast, limitless opportunity, the sense that everything is possible, possible even to frail, pluricellular man, if only he can secure the factor, *time*.

But the complex intimate structure or material composition of the protoplasmic substance, product as it is of long-standing telluric conditions which for ages have modified protoplasm in a peculiar manner, becomes permanently bent, formed and given over to life and growth in a particular mode. Oak and pine protoplasm cannot now probably become anything else; the oak must be an oak for all time to come, and the pine a pine, and certain hopeless folk think that man must die man. Oak and pine would probably perish sooner than reproduce anything else. So of most genera of plants and animals on earth, at present. But not all. On this rock split the elder Agassiz: he said, all. But some genera, or species, have always retained a certain primordial mutability and power to go higher, — among these, man, or at least some families of men. But the ages of development in the "cell," which makes that cell grow brain instead of pine, have stored up the data of insistent heredity. The innumerable atomparticles have grouped and arranged themselves in mazy series; and only altered conditions, acting on them through perhaps equal epochs of time, can permanently change them.

Better than any man of his generation, Agassiz recognized the now immutable "permanence of types" in many orders of vertebrata, orders which have long passed their developmental epoch and sunk into a Mongolian impassivity beyond the possibility of a renaissance. His exhaustive study of the fishes tended to confirm these opinions, — opinions which were correct for the fishes.   Thence he reasoned that what is unchangeable must have been created, or have come upon the earth, as we see it ; in a word, that there have been special creations of terrestrial fauna.

But to-day we recognize not only both the permanence of types, but that occasional priceless out-crop of developmental energy in protoplasm which still leads us to hope that evolution is not a " lost art " on the earth.

Investigation now interests itself with the intimate physical co-relatives of this permanence and of this developability, seeking to discover how one dot of living matter may contain the in-wrought product of millions of years of life to the end that it shall grow oak, while another dot, indistinguishable from the first beneath the strongest microscopic power, contains the equally long handiwork of ages to the end that it shall grow pine, or brain.   Into these diverse dots, the biologist would peep as adown two divergent vistas of matter, or of the universe, the far ends of which open back into the early dawn of terrestrial life.   For of such protoplasm as first stirred on earth's primitive sea-shores there is probably none now to be found.   All is old and earth-worn, bearing in its bosom the marks of its million centuries of struggle and toil, — a grand and yet a terrible legacy of heredity for the future.   If we could learn to read it, we might decipher in this soft web of sentient matter the whole past history of the globe since the first early, helpless creatures left their sinuous trails in primordial slime.   And the future Daniels of biological science will yet read the hand-writing there.

Growth is a law of living matter ; and on the earth's

surface protoplasm is capable under ordinarily favorable circumstances of increasing its bulk much more rapidly than it wastes, or dies.

It is able to conserve energy. A " cell " is capable of raising up a greater amount of non-living matter into the living condition, than it loses from the living condition by the act of so doing. In a word, it can grow, or increase its bulk. No "cell" can grow without expenditure of energy and a corresponding shrinkage of its protoplasm; but it may incorporate particles faster than it loses them, and multiply in numbers.

The only limit to such growth is the capacity of the earth as a field for life. It constantly sustains as much matter in the living condition as it has room for in the as yet imperfect and not fully developed state of its vital capacity. The various modes, or genera and species of living things, moreover, mutually limit and restrict each other. But for animals, plants would probably overrun the earth to the full extent of its standing room; but for some species of animals, others would increase inordinately. A single pair of rabbits in Australia in twenty years would have overrun the island-continent. Bacteria, in a barrel of sweet apple-juice, propagate at a rate of which no conception can be given in figures. Were the visible universe a barrel of apple-juice, these micro-organisms would fill it, twelve millions of them in every cubic centimeter of it; and within a month thereafter — having meantime developed micro-tigers, -wolves, -bears, -lions, -sharks, and perhaps micro-men, which had fought, torn, devoured and may be worshipped and philosophized — would all have perished in the sterilized liquid, save perhaps a few grim, acetic "nitrogenists" who had discovered the art of "working backwards," and hoisting "potential" up from "no potential."

The point of interest concerning this is that, given favorable conditions, with no checks to its growth, the tiniest dot of protoplasm might convert all the matter of the universe into protoplasm! or in other words, ¹ when once a *modicum* of matter, never so small, has entered the living condition, it has the power to draw an infinite quantity of contiguous matter into the same life-expressing combination, and continue the process indefinitely. It is as if the universe of matter were combustible and the dot of protoplasm, introduced into it, were a spark of fire, — with this important difference, however, that growth of living matter implies the raising up of matter to higher degrees of complexity, or the storing up of potential energy in matter, the reverse of igneous combustion. While we cannot affirm that growth of protoplasm is creative of energy, it is certainly conservative of energy in a manner elsewhere and otherwise unknown.

In protoplasm, a higher or more primary attribute of matter, to wit, *sentience*, appears to make heat, light, and kindred modes of energy its servants and to successfully stem the ordinary katabolic effects of combustion. Our present conception of matter is that, while it is manifestly not all in the living condition at present, it is yet capable from its sentient constant of being universally in the living condition, and constituting a literally *living* universe ; this in opposition to the elder hypothesis that life is a foreign force injected into dead matter by a supernatural agent.

In past ages of the world, noticeably the Carboniferous, a far greater quantity of matter has been in the living condition at one and the same time, than at present; the indications are that there have been periods when the continents sustained twenty times more vegetable protoplasm, year by year, than during the present era. From age to age the quantity has varied in accord with the terrestrial conditions.

The great cycle of intimate development, of which the living substance has been the theatre and storehouse of subjective effects, has also had the effect to limit and restrict the quantity of protoplasm which can find foothold on the earth at any given time, in later ages. Oak protoplasm is more exclusive and demands a better field than kelp or fern protoplasm; and all animal protoplasm is less easily supported and requires *pabulum* of a more refined variety than plant protoplasm. Mammals, too, have higher requirements than reptiles and the lower orders of animals. In general, the development which life on earth has given protoplasm may be said to restrict its ability to grow. Honey bees will not increase as fast as house flies; men will not multiply as rapidly as rabbits; the intimate nature of pine and human protoplasm requires a wider field for growth and taxes the vital resources of the globe more exhaustively.

What is to be the future of living matter on the earth? The question involves several biological problems which are already beginning to occupy the attention of those who study and think on these topics.

For example, will a genus of plant or animal protoplasm, as an oak or a horse, when once it has attained the acme of its terrestrial development, remain *permanent* age after age, as good as ever, so long as the terrestrial conditions remain unchanged? Does it, from some intimate protoplasmic law of its development, dependent on extra-mundane causes, tend to rise to a certain acme or zenith of developed excellence and then decline, regardless of the conditions about it? This is a problem which manifestly concerns the intimate structure of the protoplasm itself. Will the genus *elephas* remain an elephant as long as the earth continues in its present condition, or is the genus itself describing a cycle of development which rises to its zenith of elephantine excellence and as surely returns to a nadir?

We do not yet know of these things. We have learned only that by bettering the conditions, for a few years, at least, an apparent improvement may be made in certain genera of animals, like the horse, sheep, and ox, which reached what has been thought to be the acme of their race development in a former epoch. Nothing conclusive has here been established; and in regard to those races of animals which once inhabited the earth and have become extinct, we have much evidence that they perished from changed conditions, rather than from an "old age" of race. That certain genera of animals, both insects and vertebrata, have culminated from an evolutionary point of view and ceased to evince any change for the better, we have abundant evidence. It is doubtful whether a single genus or species of all earth's numerous experiments in living things can be cited as really progressive at present in the ordinary organic sense. The human race is no longer progressive from the corporeal standpoint. The only tissue of the human organism which has not already reached type limits is the nervous and cere-

bral tissue. There is still growth and organic progress
in brain, corresponding to the growth of intelligence and
the acquisition of knowledge. A new order of things is
inaugurated in this direction. The earth having ceased
to offer new conditions in the way of climate and fresh
distributions of land and water, developmental progress
has become restricted to nerve and brain tissue; and
we find growing out of this a possibility that man will,
himself, do what the earth no longer does for him; to
wit, change the terrestrial conditions to suit himself and
become the arbiter of his own future development.

But these questions concern rather the intimate
structure of protoplasm and the life of the cell. From
this our first and outer point of view, the aspect presented by the great cortex of living matter on the surface of the earth is one of constant flux, with both local
and secular increase and decrease. The picture is of a
vast volume of matter alternately entering and leaving
the living condition, obedient to cosmic law. And the
impression conveyed is, that, given certain conditions,
any and all the matter in the universe may become
living matter.

II.

THE CELL OF LIFE.

THE word " cell" as a name for the little measures of
protaplasm in which, if we may credit the geological
records in the rocks, life first began on the earth, is a
term which has come to us from the older biologists,
bestowed at a time when the nature of these vital units
was less perfectly understood than at present. It is now
of the nature of a misnomer, but is still retained, for
the reason that no term sufficiently definitive has been
found with which to replace it; for there needs to be
set forth in the new term something more than the fact
of a tiny modicum of protoplasm which absorbs pabulum and secretes formed matter, — such, for example,
as is conveyed in the ofttimes suggested terms, " plastid "
and "bioplast." For the thing to be defined is, in
reality, a living creature, an individual life, a self-
centring, sentient being.   Such a " cell " is to the human
organism what the citizen is to the nation, and it is
because the term " cell " conveys some idea of a separate
life that it possesses a certain vitality in practical use,
and will persist till better defined.

" Vital unit " is deemed too mathematical, as is also
"monad," and *corpuscle* is otherwise and specially used ;
biad would, I suppose, be considered too classical to
generally recommend itself, and we shall go on saying
cell, no doubt, till some genius, in a moment of in-
spiration, attending some grand new discovery touch-

ing this wonderful matter of life, shall triumphantly re-christen it.

The cell of life was formerly regarded much in the light of a *modicum* of pure protoplasm, which latter substance in turn was supposed to be structureless, composed of the six so-called elements, — oxygen, hydrogen, nitrogen, carbon, sulphur, phosphorus.

We now know that a cell may be something very complex. It is, in all probability, the seat of a well-nigh infinite organization of the sentient, living particles, aggregated, in-wrought, and collocated upon a plane of growth and development far beneath the reach of the microscope at present. Not otherwise could it be the theatre of such hereditary effects as we now clearly perceive it to be : effects which have been garnerèd there during many millions of years, not one of which seems ever to have been really lost, or fails, even after centuries of passivity, to be able to reappear.

The writer is one who sees reason to think that protoplasm is a substance which, if its constitution could be discerned, would be seen to contain a material fabric, corresponding to every change and every experience of its ancestry since the first fortuitous little dot of living matter first stirred and felt the thrill of subjective being on the earth. Or even, it may be, that the terrestrial living matter hails originally from some other globe in space, coming here as a hard little spore across cosmic space. Yet even that little spore might contain the physically wrought-out record of a whole prior world of life, the cycle of which had long ago been described and closed in catastrophism.

For we know that the size of the particles of universal matter cannot be greater than the one-sextillionth of an inch in diameter; that a cell of protoplasm of ordinary bulk must contain not less than a million duodecillions of such particles. That these "maximum" particles are the real atoms of matter is so wholly improbable, moreover, that few physicists would deem the hypothesis rash or incredible which portrayed them as of planetary size compared with the actually atomic attenuations of matter.

These figures and symbols are but introduced to picture, in some faint degree, the possibilities which there are in a cell of protoplasm for the storage of hereditary effects and the strong probability that it actually is such a storehouse; in a word, that one cell of protoplasm produces human brain while another produces oak bark, by reason of an ancestral constitution vastly diverse and long-derived. When our microscopic powers shall be sufficiently perfected for minute determination, these cells will be discovered to have within them the material data upon which all these diversities found.

The contents of the cell of life, however, by no means appear wholly structureless under our present powers of amplification. The contained protoplasm is often seen to be of granular aspect. Visible in most cells, too, both in unicellular and pluricellular life, there is a nucleus and often a nucleolus.

Of the many theories, more or less well-supported, as to the origin and nature of the nuclear body in cells, that appears best evidenced which regards it as originally an organ of unicellular life of the character of a generative organ, or at least concerned in reproductive growth; and that its appearance in the tissues of mammals is, in one sense, a survival from unicellular life. Yet while the nucleus, as seen in

animal tissues, may still be concerned in the intimate
process of reproduction and necessary to this animal
function, it should yet be regarded in the light of a
surviving method, having its origin not so much in the
economy of pluricellular life as in the hard, early struggles of unicellular life. At that early epoch, as we
conjecture, the nucleus was developed as a kind of
inner repository for that life that suffered constant det-
riment from the erosive agencies about it ; in order to
conserve experience and preserve individuality, it was
necessary to have a modicum of the living matter better
protected and apart from the tumult of digestive action
and assimilation. The varieties and curiosities observed in the nucleus are best explained when it is
thus regarded, — namely, as a survival organ from the
unicellular type of life.

Still further as to the structure of the protoplasm
within the cell, certain observers claim that they are
able to discern in it the appearance of a network of
contractile filaments, and hold that it consists of a delicate *reticulum* in a fluid matrix, capable of contraction
and elongation.

A reticular arrangement of the living substance is
certainly not visible in many cells, particularly in unicellular creatures. On the other hand, there are numerous protozoans in which a filamentous, contractile, and
even projectile and prehensile condition of the outer
protoplasmic layer is as certainly present. In animal
tissues, particularly adolescent tissue, the component
cells are often, perhaps constantly, connected together
by protoplasmic spikules or tendrils, and there is sometimes an appearance of intracellular filaments, as if the
connecting filament or tendril from one cell extended

quite through a neighbor cell and crossed other similar filaments from other cells, entering at different points and angles. The present writer has been unable to distinguish anything more than this, and has been inclined to regard these tendril-like emanations and combinations as the archetype of a nervous system.

There is little doubt, however, that the protoplasmic tendrils connect the millions of cells in a tissue, or organ, in a manner to communicate sensation from cell to cell, and that it is for this purpose that they reach forth and affiliate. They must hence be an important auxiliary to the nerve and brain tissue for the derivation of sensation from the cells which are the intimate seats of life. What, in the blood-circulatory, the capillaries are to the arterioles and veinlets, these protoplasmic threads and filaments, connecting cell to cell, are to the small nerves. And even as the capillaries are the most essential parts of the vascular system, so this intercellular network of living matter may be quite as essential to the nervous system ; since it unites the otherwise insulated unicellular units of the organism in one mutually sentient body. And in the case of the nervous and brain tissue, this protoplasmic sentient bond between the component cells of the " gray matter " manifestly underlies individuality, and renders personality possible in the continent mass of the encephalon.

The cell of life presents various other appearances and phases. It often contains non-living substances which are plainly out of place there, also bubbles, vacuoles, and tiny lacunes of water.

The impression will be found to grow that cells, as they occur, are far from typically perfect, and often exhibit abnormalities. It is to the intimate molecular

structure, or composition of the living substance itself,
that we shall have to look for the explanation of vital
phenomena, rather than to these grosser forms and
movements which protoplasm assumes and evinces in
the cell, as we at present view it. For nucleus, granules,
and contractile threads are but the grosser mechanical
manifestations of an arrangement of sentient particles on
a more esoteric plane of matter.   There may even be
sentient combinations within these combinations, nay
others more intimate still, ere we reach that vivific
plane where a sentient particle, or atom, is able to
move in response to its own subjective sentience and
conscious desire, and thus inaugurate motion in the
universe.   None the less, we must ultimately reach that
plane — the vital plane — where matter, any matter,
matter universally, begins to *move* from the impulse of
a subjective sentience.

It is not designed here, to open *in extenso* the much-
debated question whether matter *feels* before it moves
and moves as a result of feeling ; or *vice versa*, whether
matter is first moved extraneously, and being moved
begins to live.   Nor is *feeling*, in the physiological
sense, what is here meant.

Ultimately there can be but one conclusion reached,
namely, that matter moves from its subjective side ;
and that the interesting process which we term living,
results from first, subjectivity, then motion.   This initial
sentience of matter has existed from the beginning of
things, and when matter finds itself in the peculiar,
mobile combination of protoplasm, it is able to begin
there to overcome the terrestrial resistance to motion.

The question, whenever and however raised, always
brings the investigator around to the same point and

discloses the same necessity for a purely, personal decision on his part,— which of two opposed conceptions of cosmos he will choose as his own. He must answer for himself according to his light.

Is matter radically inert and dead, forced to move by a power foreign and primarily separate from it? Or is matter fundamentally sentient and alive, and the universe self-actuating?

There is not much that can help the questioner here, save the widest possible knowledge of nature.

If the universe is self-actuating, then matter moves from an inner sentient impulse.

If it is a dead, inert mass, actuated by a power, apart and separate from it, then the matter in protoplasm is first moved and exhibits life afterwards. The latter is the present theological doctrine, so far as that doctrine may be said to comprehend the question.

Is the universe of matter a living self-actuating universe? Or is it a dead and inert one, driven amain through space and time by a power not in it, nor of it, but launched upon it from some unknown point outside it?

We have no ambition to be polemic, and merely remark that this is the Mont St. Jean of theology and science.

Given now our cell, with its nucleus, its granules and vacuoles, let us go on to observe what actually takes place within it, as it lives and manifests that peculiar and nowhere else observed faculty of self-movement, which immediately rivets our attention as neither mechanical nor chemical, but vital; and which at once strikes the kindred chord within us, the sense of kinship and of sympathy, as something not lifeless, but living, like ourselves, with sensibility, wants, hopes,

fears, and an ever expressed desire for happiness as a
result of its struggle for existence : that sense of veri-
similitude with ourselves which renders it impossible
to look down the tube of a microscope and watch even
the tiniest bacterium, as he starts to run, or swim,
pauses, hesitates, gets frightened, changes his mind and
starts off on a different course, without the sudden strong
conviction that here is a small brother of us all, who is
having a hard time of it and who wins our pity when he
comes to grief, or gets mauled or swallowed by some
bigger fellow ; and our sympathy or admiration when
he adroitly escapes his enemy and secures a choice
mouthful for himself out of the great universal fund of
pabulum for which we are all, as well as he, struggling
to get our share.

There is now good reason for asserting that the
nucleus is that central, most intensely vivific portion of
the cell contents, which presides over nutrition, growth,
and hence reproduction — which is a mode of growth.
A stream of food particles entering the cell through the
cell wall, or envelope of the living mass, will flow
through the outer portion of protoplasm, and seems not
to be wholly transformed into protoplasm, till it has
entered, or at least come in contact with the nucleus.
But once having come into full contact with the nucleus,
the process of transformation from the condition of
food to living protoplasm appears to have become a
fact ; and the current of particles, now no longer food,
but protoplasm, turns and moves outwardly, toward the
periphery of the cell, sometimes seeming to bear along
with it the older protoplasm, sometimes appearing to
flow in a distinct current. Approaching the periphery,
it apparently becomes de-vitalized, as if the individual

life of the cell could not exist save within the circumference of a certain radius from the centre, and relapses from the living condition to the proteid condition as a cell product.

It is in this circuit of the stream of food particles, inward to the centre of the cell and outward to its circumference, to form cell products, that the mystery of life is involved.

What does this transmutation of lifeless pabulum to living protoplasm signify? What is it that has been done? Proteid molecules, such as all protoplasm consists of when killed, have returned to life. There has been a resurrection, — a rising from the dead.

Living protoplasm is a more complex compound, and more continent of energy than lifeless, proteid matter ; more units of potential work are contained in it. The food particles, during their passage to the centre of the nucleus, have, by *some power* resident in protoplasm, been raised and re-grouped upon a higher level of complexity. In their passage back to the periphery, and their fall to the lifeless condition of cell products, or proteid matter, power is generated. The whole amount of bodily power is thus derived, in fact. It results from the process of devitalization, and is to all appearance accomplished by the agency of oxygen imported by the red corpuscles of the blood from the external air.

But the longer we examine it the more evident it becomes that this latter derivation of power by oxygenation, during the de-vitalization of living protoplasm, must be regarded as the reverse step only, — the *fall of the weight* raised up by vitalization. In a word, that, instead of one, two distinct series of phenomena take place simultaneously in every living cell, namely, a flowing inward and upward to the nucleus of a current of proteid matter, which is vivified and charged with energy by so doing, from contact with the resident living matter of the cell, and a flowing outward and downward of a stream of living protoplasm, which *loses life* and *thereby gives out power.* The latter process is manifestly chemism, and is accomplished by the action of energies which we know as chemical. This chemism, indeed, is what many — in fact, the most — physiologists have mistaken for the whole function of the cell. In reality it is the least important function. The really important function of the living cell is the raising up of the weight, or the generation of power by the act of vitalization.

The power to do this, we say, resides in the original living matter of the cell, which is obtained by inheritance from earliest and lowliest ancestry. It is quite conceivable, indeed, that, given one primordial cell, originating from the chance collocation of carbon, oxygen, hydrogen, and nitrogen particles, during the early terrestrial tumult, the entire surface of the earth may have become covered with living forms; that every species of plant and animal may have arisen from it.

The protoplasm of plants and vegetation generally, which is not compelled to accomplish locomotion, possesses the ability to raise vast quantities of low-grade matter, to wit, carbon dioxide, water, and ammonia, directly upward into starch, fat oil, and vegetable albumen. Far greater power in this respect resides in vegetable than in animal protoplasm. Given H_2O, $N H_3$, and $C O_2$ in infinite quantity, with a modicum of living vegetable protoplasm through which it may continuously

pass, and if time be given for the process, there is practically no limit to the quantity of starch, sugar, fat,
gluten, and cellulose which may be produced. Given
a sufficient time period, indeed, it is conceivable that a
single cell of protoplasm might have raised up the entire quantity of starch, sugar, fat, and gluten at present
existing on the earth. Nor is there any reason to think
that such a cell might not, under favorable conditions,
go on thus storing up power through infinite time.

Hence, it is manifest that behind this cell of protoplasm, displaying such exhaustless capacity for work,
there must be a commensurate power supply. For no
one supposes the cell to be more than a self-sustaining, self-repairing instrument or collocation of matter,
through which the energy of the material particles acts.
What then is the nature of the power behind it or from
what source does it emanate?

To the writer there appears to be but one answer.

It emanates outward from the inner *penetralia* of
matter, from an inner plane of material combination.
Protoplasm acts as a vehicle, or a medium of conduc-
tion, so to speak, for the liberation of this power outward into the grosser plane of chemism as kinetic
energy. This inner shrine, or intimate plane of matter,
we may term the vital plane. Here the sentient
particles are self-motive. Here the initial sentience —
which is the mainspring of the universe — is able to
express itself in terms of motion; the particles feel and
move. This initial sentience of the ultimate particles
of universal matter may be regarded as a static property, an archaic attribute, a constant in nature, — in
the sense at least that it is here renewed constantly in
the grand cycle of universal phenomena.

From this sentient plane the "natural forces" of matter emerge, and to this plane they return.

The little measure of protoplasm contained in a cell offers an outlet to the intimate sentient energy of matter universally. Protoplasm touches down to the sentient plane. In protoplasm, the static sentient property can stir contiguous particles, draw them within the bond of sentient relationship and collocate them one with another, so that they, too, can stir and move other particles. In living, the modicum or cell of protoplasm first grows to the terrestrial cell size, and then, when this limit is reached, either deposits " formed matter " (dead protoplasm) around the boundary of the cell, or else divides to form new cells. But the point here to be kept in view is, that an exhaustless source of power from the sentient side of matter finds an outlet into ordinary terrestrial matter through the medium of the protoplasmic cell. That such a vital plane of matter, where *the sentient particles are self-motive*, really exists and that upon it founds the great doctrine of Free Will in man, is the position here adopted, and one which will be given a more full demonstration in future.

The purpose in the present paper, however, is to set forth the fact of the intimate seat of personality in the cell; or in other words, to point out that the cell is not only a *modicum* of protoplasm, but the instrumentality of a *self*, an ego, a personal being. In a cell a certain number of millions or sextillions of material particles, each one of which is a sentient particle and in lowly degree, a self-sentient particle, are so collocated that they blend their sentience in one and form an individual life ; even as in pluricellular organisms, millions of these individual cells merge their personal lives in the life and intellect of an animal or a man. The cell is a bond of sentient particles. Moreover, so far from being simple homogeneous dots of living matter, most cells, either of unicellular or pluricellular life, are of the nature of very complex organisms, the repositories of a vast ancestral experience.

III.

THE SENTIENT CONSTANT OF MATTER.

WE are able to gain mathematical knowledge of particles of matter so minute that ten quadrillions of them would not weigh the thousandth part of a grain, nor when aggregated be visible to the eye.

We know that particles exist so small that a stream of them may fly off constantly from a mass for a quarter of a century without diminishing the weight of the mass by so much as the hundredth part of a grain; yet from their physical behavior we know that each one of these vagrant particles possesses weight, chemical properties, and the power to produce sentient effects. In a word, throughout the length and breadth of cosmos, there has never been discovered a particle of the universal substance of things so small that it does not possess these properties and powers. Such an undowered particle, indeed, would be something more than an anomaly. It would be a nonentity. We could not know it as matter; for we have no knowledge of matter with which there is not included a contingent of energy. Inert matter does not exist, so far as known; and it is plain, too, that no knowledge of it could ever be obtained by science, or by human sense, if it did exist. Hence it is out of the question and out of the province even of " revelation."

The scholastic conception of inert matter and " original world-atoms " upon which a " world energy " operates is a very crude one, derived from the merely visual inertia or stability of terrestrial matter in the gross. Such "inertia" of matter is perceived only by virtue of latent properties which transcend the very conception of inertia. If wholly inert, matter would be invisible, imperceptible to touch or feeling, and outside of any possibility of becoming known to us. Hence to speak of inert matter, or inert atoms, is to stultify one's self.

In the same category fall all those abortive definitions which have been attempted of energy or force. No one can define energy in terms which do not include matter. *Vice versa*, matter can not be defined in terms exclusive of energy; and this for the best of reasons, namely, that the human intellect can obtain no conception of inert matter, or "pure" energy. The similes on which all such definitions have been projected were conceived by aid of the very constants *which the definitions attempted to exclude!*

Hence we set down as one of the premises of this inquiry, that matter and energy are indissoluble, or what comes to the same, that we have not and never can have knowledge of one separate from the other. And here it may be added, incidentally, that this later doctrine of matter and energy as components, outranks both the accusation of materialism on one hand and of spiritism on the other.

If this conception be as true and as unassailable as we conceive it to be, every particle of the unnumbered millions of particles which enter a cell of living matter as pabulum, and are assimilated and, for the time being, take their places in it as protoplasm, brings with it its inseparable quota of energy; and, moreover, while in

the living condition, this energy is exhibited as subjective sentience. But departing out of the cell, as
formed matter or waste, it carries its native and inseparable measure of energy with it. Sentient in human
protoplasm, it may ere long appear again, perhaps, in
plant protoplasm, or bacteria, or never again, or not
for a thousand or a million years. For it may exist
in earth, water, or air, or fire-dust, till solar systems
change form and grow again; yet, whenever it shall
enter protoplasm, it would still exhibit life.

As to the nature of this orginal *modicum* of energy
which the particles of matter possess, no one can give
it name or say what it is in terms that adequately de-
scribe it. Scientists define it as *vis viva*, energy,
dynamic property, power, force — according to the
way in which it is conditioned and manifested. All the
elder school of scientific writers discriminated between
physical and vital energy. It was not easy then
to see that the impulse which exhibited itself as
gravitation could possibly be the same as that which
stirred in protoplasm as life. In the same manner the
philosopher of an earlier date could not conceive of
heat as a mode of motion, but pictured it as "caloric,"
— something *sui generis*.

Only gradually has this philosophical and scientific
polytheism been *monotheized*, so to speak, and the
unity of the universal energy been accepted as the true
faith.

With wider light and from the broader view, biology
can now confidently teach that the property which the
particles of universal matter exhibit as sentience in
protoplasm is the same which, in combustion, is displayed as heat and light, or in electrolysis as electric

tension, or in falling bodies as gravitation, or in the rifle shot as momentum, or in the sun's vast molar mutations as all of these together. We no longer fear that we shall lose dignity, or become materialistic, if we rank our intellects with heat and light. Heat and light may be as "divine" as we! Potential divinity, indeed, is on all sides of us. The meanest clod contains it. One particle is as divine as another. All are peers. It is merely a question of how long and how carefully the particles — each with its eternal inheritance of divinity — have had opportunity to arrange themselves in relation one with another in the cell of living matter. A cell of the human brain is a highly-wrought and intimately constituted congeries of particles which have been getting into their present condition of excellent sentient relationship during a hundred millions of years. We conceive of such a cell as containing what, mathematically, would appear an innumerable number of particles, brought rank on rank, series on series, and system on system, and in such delicate poise and balance, one to another, that every one of these millions of particles stands sentiently related to all, and that, from this fine mutual reciprocity, sense which has been elevated to intellect arises.

But any particle of matter is capable and qualified to enter such a cell, live in it as a peer of all the rest for a time, and, departing thence, enter other combinations and exhibit the energy which it recently displayed in intelligence, as light, or heat, or other motion.

There is, indeed, a constant inrush of particles into such a cell, and a corresponding exodus as formed matter and waste. But the excellence of the inherited mutual relationship of particle to particle is preserved, or deteriorates but slowly and secularly ; hence the cell preserves its individuality, although its component particles are constantly shifting, entering and escaping in streams on all sides. Such a picture every cell of living matter presents so long as it lives, and it is from a long observation of these phenomena that the present doctrine of life is conceived ; namely, that any particle of oxygen, hydrogen, nitrogen, carbon, and sulphur, in cosmos, will do equally as well as another for the exhibition of life ; that these particles may alternately enter and leave a cell of protoplasm a hundred times, yet always display the same measure of energy when drawn into the sentient brotherhood, and that this capacity to *live* is from a property inherent in them, which they can be deprived of by no known means, and which no application of external force can either slacken or intensify.

This quotum of energy is what we mean by the sentient constant of matter.

The terms " sentient constant," " sentient property," and "inherent sentience of universal matter," as employed in these papers, signifying the initial energy of the intimate particles of matter, is not free from objection, nor yet in accord with the secondary use of the words, *sentient* and *sentience*. None the less, it is the best word term, taking into consideration exactly what needs to be expressed, in view of the present biological aspects of matter, that has thus far suggested itself.

The term " living matter " has been used to designate a portion of ordinary matter the particles of which, for the time, chance to be in such a condition of mutual relationship that their native sentience is able to give rise to subjective phenomena.

According to this conception of matter, the sentient

constant of the material particles is their primary and inseparate component, that factor, property, or ingredient, which constitutes them matter as we know it. Hence, we allude to the *sentience* of matter as a constant, meaning the *ability*, potency, or capacity of matter to live. We further conceive of this sentient constant as the original world impulse, by virtue of which motion is evinced and all phenomena are exhibited. The conception is, that intrinsically and fundamentally the universe is a *living* universe, not a lifeless mass driven forward by an external, extrinsic agent. As to the origin of the sentient constant of matter, or what it is ultimately, nothing is attempted in the line of explanation or definition. It is seen to be a component property of the most minute particle of universal matter and seen to possess the *elements* of sentience. With the words " elemental sentience " our conception of it stops and can advance no farther.

It is not to be inferred, however, that this definition represents minute particles of matter as intelligent or personal, in the sense that living creatures are so. Animals are long-matured resultants of protoplasmic life. They vary in intelligence according to the excellence of their organisms. An amoeba can scarcely be said to approximate a dog or a man in intelligence. Similarly, the sentient difference between an amoeba and a particle of unorganized matter, is no doubt far wider than that between an amoeba and a man.

We do not conceive that this sentient property is other than the property exhibited in the gravitation of matter, or in chemical action, or in any of the so-called natural forces. We see no reason to think that all phenomena are not from one and the same source of energy. In other words, gravity and the kinetic modes of energy in cosmos originate in a sentient impulse in matter.

It is likely and probable that all chemism is attended by a low degree of sentience. Not the pain or pleasure of the organized developments of living matter, since these include personality, but a certain low grade of sensation. The universe seems, indeed, to be *feeling* its way forward in time and space according to certain very lowly and rudimentary, yet enormously massive, perceptions of what is right and wrong, true and false, good and bad. And while there is nothing in the totality of its phenomena, as we observe them, which leads us to infer that it possesses a high order of intelligence, it yet inspires us with a certain degree of confidence that these humble, but immensely voluminous perceptions, purblind and impersonal as they appear, will not in the end and on the whole go wrong. Such, I think, is the impression which the universe gives to all who make wide and dispassionate observation; namely, that its vast energies make, or tend to make, for good, and are voluminous and strong enough, in the end, to prevail over accidental evil. There may be, probably are, globes of matter in space where this orbic benevolence is more perfectly displayed than on the earth. There are astronomic reasons why the earth can hardly be regarded as a comparatively well-favored globe, considered as a *habitat* for personalized forms of living matter. Life here — animal life — struggles against an enormous physical resistance. To live on the surface of our earth at present implies a grim death-grapple with adverse conditions. Protoplasm, indeed, wastes or dies in its effort to grow or live, with a rapidity and distress which are appalling to contemplate. Owing to the hard terrestrial conditions we have become organized to live only as we die, or are disintegrated. It is by no means an ideal theatre of life; and there is a great deal of prayer and despair along the line of our developmental struggle. What looks to be best and most beautiful, is most frequently crushed out ruthlessly. Not ruthlessly, if that word be used as a reproach for cruelty. Nature protects as far as it knows and perceives. There is no wanton cruelty. There is no immoral neglect from nature. It is only that the great, lowly-sentient mass on which we live and the vaster globes about which it ponderously wheels, are but little conscious of our personal fortunes. So far as they feel and know they smile and protect. But we must not expect too much.

It would seem rather wonderful and anomalous if, somewhere in space, on globes better conditioned to sustain life, organisms, animals, beings superhuman, had not arisen from living matter to a height of intelligence surpassing man. Analogy would lead us to fancy that such are able to watch the earth from afar and, in the perfection of their visual or telescopic powers, mark us at our toil. Such beings might, we can imagine, at least be able to assist us, or "reveal" some truth that would aid us. But on the whole, there is not the slightest evidence that any aid of this sort has ever come to the earth out of space.

The ordinary conception of matter is a wholly superficial and erroneous one. Matter is conceived of as " dirt," as " earthy," as contemptible. This idea comes from ignorance of what matter is. When the biologist asserts that life is an organized derivative from a primary property of universal matter, theologian and sectary are at once shocked at what seems to them a blasphemy; namely, that life has arisen from dirt! It is plain that this revulsion of their sensibilities springs from a low estimate of matter. There is no such thing in *cosmos* as "dirt," in this sense. Yet the odium in the accusation, "materialist" and "atheist," all founds in this erroneous popular idea. To the mind of a well-instructed biologist, on the contrary, matter is a sublime mystery.

Whence it came or whitherward it moves, none can answer. It is the unknown. We feel, see, and study certain of its phases, but of its origin, or destiny, we know nothing as yet.

Not from lifeless atoms then, not from "dirt" are our intellects arisen, but from a sentient *substance* which fills all space and endures through all time, indestructible, immortal, the type and symbol of omnipotence. What grander origin could humanity claim for itself!

Even our present scanty knowledge of matter enables us to perceive that such are its attributes; and ever as the horizon of our science broadens and the clouds of our ignorance lift, we are led to regard matter with new awe and greater reverence. Fresh from the mutations and destructive catastrophes of a thousand world-deaths, it emerges ever new with the same onimpotent power to create afresh. Yesterday, to-day, forever, it is the same exhaustless well-spring of motion, beauty, feeling, and life.

Life arises from the sentient constant of matter; the protoplasmic cell is a more or less permanent aggregation of particles whose sentient endowment is static and eternal; the problem of prolonged life, both in unicellular and pluricellular creatures, lies in preserving the cell from destruction, injury, and undue waste. Greatly prolonged life, immortal life even, is possible, potential. Immortality, indeed, is clearly foreshadowed in the sentient constant of the material particles of which the earth, the universe, is composed. These ever-sentient, never-dying particles furnish the basis for it.

It becomes, therefore, a question of preserving the cell, the self, from harm, from preponderant waste, from accidents, and from the ravages of hostile forms of life :— all essentially vulgar causes of death, none of which touch, or *ever* can touch, the sentient well-spring of life in atomic matter; and all directly amenable to human effort to ameliorate and remove.

IV.

WHENCE AND WHAT IS THE INTELLECT OR "SOUL"?

HISTOLOGICALLY speaking, the human body is a confederation of thirty or more genera and species of minute living creatures, commonly termed "cells," whose ancestry was the unicellular life of the ancient earth.

The cell of life may now in strictest truth be defined as a microscopic creature, composed of living matter, or protoplasm, protected by the non-living products of the same ; nor can it be regarded otherwise than as an individual being, possessed of a personal sense and, even in highly developed pluricellular organisms, of a considerable degree of autonomy.

It is well to remember that the great bulk of terrestrial life is still unicellular, and that pluricellular animals are to be regarded as a later and by no means yet complete development from unicellular life. If the reader has access to large well-illustrated text-books, or atlases of zoölogy, it will be worth the while to spend an hour, at this point, reviewing the numerous varieties, species and orders of this wonderful unicellular life of the globe.   Even the condensed articles on this subject in the "Encyclopedia Britannica" will convey an idea and give some conception of it.

Passing forward from unicellular life, an atlas of Histology, with numerous illustrations of the various orders of cells in animal tissues, will prove suggestive.

In particular should be noted the layer of large multipolar cells of the cortex of the brain, — how the protoplasmic processes or living filaments from these, rising upward to form the gray matter of the brain, blend, inter-twine, *and sentiently communicate* one with another in a manner at once wonderful and significant. It is here that the personality of a million different cells is united into one intellect or "soul."

If an attempt be made to extend the above definition of a "cell," the limits of our present knowledge are soon touched.

The protoplasm, of which the cell is composed, is a transient, easily desintegrated compound of ordinary matter, which material particles are constantly entering, and from which they as constantly emerge; that is to say, it is not these ordinary oxygen, carbon, and nitrogen particles which make protoplasm, so much as the manner in which they are grouped together; since these same particles may be otherwise associated together and no visible token of life result; and by visible life, we mean life attended by movement and protoplasmic growth. It is apparently a question of collocation, or relative position of particle to particle, allowing of a peculiar interaction and a unique expression of the primary powers of the particles.

The true terrestrial type of life was and still is unicellular; creatures consisting of a single protoplasmic cell from which are displayed all the functions, in miniature, exhibited by pluricellular creatures. These are the protozoans, the first, the standard type; nor is this type essentially changed in the metazoans, or pluricellular organisms, since the latter are merely well-confederated associations of unicellular creatures. There is indeed but one type of life on the surface of our globe, the unicellular, and this type is preserved in all forms of life.

Pluricellular organisms are a later development from unicellular life. At first the metazoans were small, simple aggregations of the protozoans; and the fact of confederation appears not even to have modified the separate unicellular lives. Each retained complete autonomy, performing all the functions of a separate life. Change of the conditions of *habitat* led to more permanent grouping and induced modification and differentiation of functions, till at length dissolution of the bond which united the several unicellular lives became impossible; and thus the way for further differentiation of functions and the evolution of compacted and organized metazoans was opened.

All the pluricellular organisms of which the human body is an eminent example, are but extensive, organized unions of unicellular life in which the type of unicellular life still distinctly persists.

It is not the purpose here to introduce illustrations, *seriatim*, of such metazoans. Survivals of very early groups are even now to be found. But as new conditions of existence occurred, from geological mutations, the primitive simplicity of the early confederations of unicellular life was modified; they took on a greater degree of permanence and grew to larger proportions; and the better to accomplish locomotion, respiration, prehension, and digestion, a division of labor became necessary; the original diverse functions of the component unicellular creatures, thus banded together, were restricted, or extended; and, as a result of a long process of such differentiation, the organisms of the larger animals and of man came to be composed, as we find them, of thirty or more different species of cells. For example, we have the muscle cells whose vital energies are devoted to the office of contraction, or vigorous shortenings of length ; connective tissue cells whose office is mainly to produce and conserve a tough fibre for binding together and covering in the organism ; bone cells whose life work it is to select and collocate salts of lime for the organic frame-work, levers and joints ; hair, nail, horn, and feather cells which work in silicates for the protection, defence and ornamentation of the organism ; gland cells whose *motif* in living has come to be the abstraction from the blood of substances which are recombined to produce "juices," needed to aid the various processes or steps of digestion ; blood cells which have assumed the laborious function of general carriers, scavengers, and repairers of the organism ; eye, ear, nasal and palate cells which have become the special artificers of complicated apparatuses for transmitting light, sound, odors and flavors to the highly sentient brain cells ; pulmonary cells which elaborate a tissue for the introduction of oxygen and the elimination of carbon dioxide and other waste products ; hepatic cells which have, in response to the needs of the organism, descended to the menial office of living on the waste products and converting them to chemical reagents, to facilitate digestion ; these and numerous other species of cells ; and lastly, most important and of greatest interest, nerve and brain cells. Most important and of greatest interest, because this genus of cells is the seat of intelligence, and has arisen to a far higher estate than that of their more lowly fellows. For intellectually man is something more than a congeries of cell tribes.   Otherwise, we should have to represent him as a huge sprawling amoeboid mass, feeling its way to food, or escaping danger by the most rudimentary acts of sensory perception.

But when we speak of a man we mean his nervous system and brain, so far as personality and intelligence are concerned.   Such reference is not generally to his muscle cells, his hepatic cells, or his blood cells, but to those of his nerves and brain, of which all the others are but the semi-conscious servants.

For it is manifest that in muscle, bone, and connective tissue we contemplate a certain degradation of typical cell life to menial estate.   The life of these genera of cells goes merely to swell the volume of *feeling*, or general sense, as distinguished from intelligence.   It is not a high order of cell life, but it gives rise to the sense of feeling voluminously.   When we speak of the intelligence, the intellect, the "soul" of man, however, we mean the life of the cells of his brain and nerves.

But how and why has this tissue, this genus of cells, — originally not different from others — assumed the ascendency and attained this regal supremacy?   Certain results from the present writer's own investigations may here be introduced as preliminary to an answer.

While attempting to determine the nature of the stimulus which is sometimes communicated to the nuclei in the walls of the blood capillaries, inciting them in case of damage to a renewed growth after long periods of inactivity, a hint was gained as to the manner, or rather the means, by which this vital stimulus is conveyed to them.   I am not about to speak of the small nerves which are often found entwined around the capillary vessels. These, indeed, carry stimuli to the capillaries, but reference is now made to interaction in a more intimate manner, to wit, that between cell and cell.

To properly set forth and illustrate this condition it is necessary to again refer to unicellular life. Beginning with the amoeboid forms of life and reviewing the protozoans, — rhizopods, ciliates, flagellates, *et als.*, we find that the cell of life, when leading a solitary, independent existence, possesses the power to throw out from its protoplasmic substance projections (pseudopodia) and filaments. In the better developed protozoans these projections assume a more or less permanent character, as cilia and flagella. By means of such voluntary or habitual projections, the unicellular creature is able to communicate with its fellows, as well as to take knowledge of surrounding objects and seize its food. Ofttimes these filaments can be quickly thrown out or retracted; they are themselves living matter, capable of feeling, and moving in response to it.

This power and this habit of projecting living filaments outward are not absent in the millions of histological cells or vital units of animal organisms. Even in bone the cells send out such communicating threads and lines which penetrate the interstices of the non-living substance and touch one another. The so-called cell wall does not confine or restrict these minute affiliations of cell contents with cell contents. Such filaments constitute a living sensory bond between cell and cell. Whether these filaments have a degree of permanency and continue projected or extended for a considerable length of time I have no certain evidence;

but even our crude straining processes exhibit them at times. It is quite likely that delicate and protoplasmic as they are, being part of the ever changeful living matter about the nucleus, these filaments are projected and retracted in response to some want or emotion of the cell; that they are not permanent appendages, but are sent forth, shortened, or prolonged, according to the stress which prompts them and the distance which they have to traverse to reach a neighbor cell.

There are appearances in cells which indicate that these out-reaching living lines sometimes traverse a neighboring cell, and that a cell may be reached and penetrated by several such filaments from a number of adjoining cells. A cell may thus be permeated and influenced by half a dozen of its fellows at one and the same moment. Most probably these delicate living tentacles may be and are often withdrawn. We can more easily believe them to be transient, since they are protoplasmic.

None the less, it is likely that the continuity of sense and the individuality of the organism depend largely on them; and that they are the sub-stratum so to speak of the nerve system, the delicate changeful ground-work of cellular intercourse on which the *ego* rests. The organism of a man, *e. g.*, is made up of many billions of cells, each a living creature. The cells, in fact, constitute the only living part of the body. They are the units of life, and it is only by virtue of the sentient filaments which they emit to each other, that a continent sentient tissue results from them.

Whether these filaments, blending and getting larger from cell to cell, constitute the radicles of the nervous system, I cannot say. Our present preparation processes are very unfavorable for tracing such continuations if they exist. The small nerves proper sometimes appear to terminate in relatively gigantic "nerve plates." It is probable that nerve cells and nerve tissue proper are a distinct genus of cells, acted upon by the cells of the contiguous tissues only after a considerable stress or tension has accumulated in a given tract and is communicated disjunctly after the manner of the electric spark. What I have seen convinces me that there is communication by means of living filaments of protoplasm between cell and cell in all the tissues when in normal condition. In no tissue is this living connection so complete as in nerve tissue and gray cerebral tissue. Not unfrequently so many of these living protoplasmic filaments enter a cell from neighboring cells as to give the cell contents, outside the nucleus, an appearance of being a network of protoplasmic threads. This is not always the case, however, and apparently depends upon the state of vital intercommunication existing in a tissue at the time when the preparation of it for the microscope was made.

This filamentous living connection of cell with cell may be the under-lying cause and the reason why billions of cells can exist as an *ego*, an individual animal, and exhibit personality. For although separate selves, they *sense* by reason of these mutual filaments each other's lives, and feel, each as his fellow feels. In a word, they are thus able all to feel as *one*.

To resume more concretely, we must conceive of the human body as made up of from five to eight hundred billions of cells; and that each cell has developed to its present condition during the million of centuries since protoplasm first appeared on the earth. For from what we already know of matter, and its well-nigh infinite attenuation, we conceive the cell of life to have within it ample room for such development; and that, if we could secure the necessary magnifying powers, we should behold it as presenting capacity for unbounded progress: a world within itself, indeed. Then contemplate the organic life of man as a union of all these diverse genera of cell lives in one, — and some conception may be gained how complicated and long-derived a result a human life actually is. The intimate arrangement of a cell of each one of these genera of cells has been and stands in the tissues to-day as a work of untold and inestimable toil, a fabric of incalculable price. Within those tiny yet augustly capacious *modica* of living matter are compressed and pent the sighs, the longings, the strivings, the despairs, the hopes, and the joys of millions of years of hapless individual effort.

Most emphatically is this true of the four pounds of brain and nerve tissue in the human organism, representing nearly sixty-five millions of cells of the genus *mens*. To be able to set forth even in outline some idea of the incomparable cost and value of the living matter in human protoplasm, is one of the recent possibilities of modern biology. It unfolds a new conception of what life really is, and makes possible a new definition of the human intellect and soul.

What we contemplate in the human organism is a vast congeries of unicellular life, sensorily united in one by *living* filaments, so that the impulse of life in one is felt throughout the others; and the sentience of one is enabled thereby to affect the sentience of another, and cause cumulative effects. How sensation is communicated, that is to say, by means of what mode, or modes of energy, whether a simple wave-motion, chemism, or electro-motive energy, it is not easy to determine. Perhaps, by a combination of modes.

Certain investigators are inclined to adopt the idea of a current of actual particles along the filaments which are the prototypes of the nerves, and in fact what may be termed *capillary* nerves ; a current, bearing particles, thus constituting a transmission of portions of one cell to another and an incorporation of one within another. By virtue of such mutual transmissions and incorporations, two, or a thousand, cells, are made to feel, act, and live as one.

Keeping in view therefore the means by which many cells are able to live in a sentient unity, or personality, we revert to the question advanced above : —

Why and how has the brain become exalted above the living matter of the other tissues of the organism?

We discover even in unicellular creatures a certain massing and condensing of the living matter along axial lines of energy, weight, and resistance. Even inside the cell and in the protoplasm itself, there may be said to be the unstable semblance of an apparatus for the application of developed power in the living matter. But such apparatus did not become permanent and organic till the union of unicellular lives into a living creature of larger dimensions had taken place.

Why such a union ever began to occur, we have not space here to suggest reasons. It is certain that it took place ; and we are now concerned to mark the results which followed it. The general purpose, as is evident, was to secure greater liberty and a broader field for development. But while this greater liberty and broader field for life was gained by a portion of the living creatures, thus combining together, cell on cell, it was for a portion only; and a part, the larger part, was rather degraded than elevated, to secure this boon for the more fortunate part.

This is one of the strange, sad phases of life in terrestrial matter, — an aspect which seems world-wide and time-long, from lowliest forms of life to the highest. A part has been raised up and attained a wonderful development, but this result has been reached at the expense of another portion which has been obliged to step downward to a lowlier lot and assume a heavier burden, that a more favored portion may step higher and bear a lighter burden.

The writer freely confesses that this aspect of protoplasmic life is one which he can find no adequate explanation of under any known system of morals; and one which more than any other has led him to doubt whether *we have really any moral code* which includes the general *morale* of nature.

The doubt is not whether there is primarily and ultimately a moral code in nature and in the universe of sentient matter, but rather that in our ignorance of the universe we have not as yet apprehended what are its real ethics.

Very soon after animals composed of many cells (metazoans) began to exist, the necessities of locomotion in the struggle for food led to the differentiation of certain tracts of cells as bone and muscle, and finally to the development of the entire apparatus for mechanical movements.

Simultaneously, too, another peculiar species of differentiation began to be necessary, namely, a special tissue, whose office should be that of inter-communica-

tion between the different associated cells and tracts of
cells which were thus assuming more and more diverse
offices, and becoming somewhat different in character,
one from another.   It was thus and for this reason that
a nervous system began to be needed and hence to
develop; for the plastic, living substance has always
shown a faculty of adapting itself to widely variant
functions and modes of living.

Certain cells began to take up the business of receiving sensory influences from outlying cells which were
hard-pressed, or in want of food, and of transmitting
such sensory influences to contiguous cells.   In short,
certain lines of internal cells began to take upon themselves the task of conveying the sensations of others
from one tract of the cellular mass to another tract, and
of interpreting the sensation received from one tract to
the comprehension of the sentience of another tract, so
that action, within its sphere of action, would ensue in
the second tract.   In addition to their own sentient
economy, these lines of cells in the incipient nervous
system took up the function of common carriers of *sense*,
and also the office of interpreters of the sensory language of one order of cells — if I may borrow the
figure — to the different language of another order.

Thus, humbly, as we conclude from observation of
low forms of life, did the nervous system, or tissue of
intelligence, begin to develop.   Primarily there was
but one or two simple thread-like lines of cells attempting the office of transmitting feeling, and succeeding
indifferently at first; but as animals increased in size,
the business of telegraphing sensation grew, and a network of lines was developed.   Sensation was going
both ways, and soon the necessity of a common centre

to which sensory influences could be brought, and thence
distributed to their proper destination, was forced upon
the nascent, sense-conveying cells, and a ganglion, or
little brain, came into existence. The confusion, too,
resulting from counter currents of feeling soon led to
the formation of double lines, — one for transmitting
sensation inward, the other for transmission outward ;
and thus the divisions of sensory and motor nerves
were inaugurated to and from the little brain centre,
which presently assumed the function of deciding upon
the merits of transmitted sensations and responding to
them by a message from its own sensibility.

Nerve ganglia multiplied, as animals increased in
bulk, and attempted larger movements ; and in time, to
avoid confusion and get business done, one ganglion was
obliged to take the lead and keep order among the other
ganglia, to decide between them when they got at vari-
ance, and, generally, to take the office of head ganglion.

Thus, in time, a larger and capitally important ganglion was raised up into prominence to perform the function of oyer and terminer ; a cerebellum and finally a
cerebrum,— a mass of highly organized cells which have,
from long use and inherited development, the capacity
for intelligent perception and thought.

In the living matter of ganglia and of brain, there is,
undoubtedly, an arrangement and relative grouping of
material particles which corresponds to the degree of
sentient elevation. Brain protoplasm would be found
to differ in delicacy and complication from bone protoplasm by as much as a brain cell is more intelligently
sentient than a bone cell. We conclude that the intellectual faculty of the living matter of the brain must
be held to rest on a basis of formation or arrangement

of the living sentient substance, and on the relationship of the particles of that substance one to another. What is true of cerebral cells is, beyond doubt, true of bone cells, muscle cells, and the cells of all the organic tissues. Their different functions result from variations in their intimate composition.

Thus, in the end, a kind or order of intellectually differentiated protoplasm was developed whose office it is to deal with sensation from all the other differentiated orders of protoplasm, and also to receive through the special sense organs impressions from the external world; to receive, convey, estimate, and decide on the merits and relative character of all these incoming sensations and perceptions, and finally to assume the responsibility of becoming arbiter and director for all its associate tissues. But, while receiving this exalted development from the necessities of its situation in the organism and accepting this regal function, it yet remains protoplasm in the cell form and living the cell life, with the usual nutritive economy, and capable of movement by the agency of chemism and, as we hold, by the passage of its sentience into will-power which directs the movements for which chemism furnishes the larger share of the motive force.

Not all, indeed, of the brain and nervous system is composed of living matter of so exalted a grade; portions of it are but the frame-work upon which the gray matter rests and by means of which it is able to act. By the tissue of intellect, as here spoken of, is meant the portion in which self-consciousness appears and intellectual processes inhere : the regal gray substance of which all the nerve fibres, trunks, and adjunctive ganglia are the instruments.

Thus we see that in the organism, containing perhaps twenty pounds of protoplasm, at least seventeen pounds have been to a certain degree degraded from the original condition, seen in unicellular life, to less sentient, special and servile offices, in order to serve and raise up to the estate of intelligence the more favored two or three pounds.

In the larger sense, the result may be said to have amply justified the means; for that result is the human intellect, in place of a mass of protoplasm of low sentient coefficient.

At first we observe a partial degradation of virgin protoplasm to a lower *status* of sensibility, as seen in cartilage, bone, sinew, connective tissue and blood; liver, spleen, and glandular tissue; cuticle, hair, nails, and teeth. By this sacrifice, support, defence and an apparatus for locomotion and mechanical work were secured, along with the facilities for assimilation and digestion of food; also vision, hearing, taste, and smell. It is upon this sub-structure, the sentience of which has been lowered, or diverted to the production of mechanical effects, that the ennobled protoplasm of intellect rests and depends.

To the gray living matter of brain and ganglia, highly elaborated and correspondingly delicate, the lowlier tissues offer protection from the cold, rough environment amidst which we live and move. Housed about by bone, hair, and hide, sustained aloft in nature by brawn which moves it at its sovereign pleasure, fed by alimentary and vascular tissue which labors incessantly that it may have prepared food brought to its door, the royal encephalon has had the opportunity to develop to intellect. Intelligence is as much the life of the brain, as contractility is the life of muscle; but it represents, and is objectively represented by, an arrangement which, compared with that of muscle protoplasm, must be marvellously delicate and elaborate. Yet but for this reduction and subjection of the muscle and bone protoplasm to secure these protective, defensive, and otherwise provident advantages, intellect could never have come into being.

Recently — since "phrenology" ran its erratic course — considerable progress has been made in "mapping" the human brain, with a view to locating the various "faculties" of the intellect; and so far as this much-needed work has progressed, the results lend strength to the several conclusions set forth in this paper.

But an important fact must not here be lost sight of, one concerning which a close study of the cell of life in human tissues enables us to speak with certainty, and one which is not without significance in an attempt to learn what the intellect, or "soul" of man really is. Even the brain is not composed wholly of living matter which is *subjective* on the side of personal intelligence; it passes by different degrees into *objective* matter. This, indeed, is the case, to some extent, even inside the most delicate and highly differentiated cell in the "gray matter." Even in the branched gray cells, there is matter which is apparently more earthy and less purely subjective than the rest. Not half, not a third, of the cerebrum is entirely the tissue of intellect. If any one tract, or division, of the brain were purely intellectual tissue, isolated by itself, we should unhesitatingly apply the term *intellect* to this tract.

From the *errata* of nutrition there are imported into the protoplasmic substance unassimilated products ("formed matter") of previous protoplasmic life, as also inorganic particles, so that it is impossible to speak of even the apparently living matter of the brain as purely intellectual tissue. It is probable that this ╡alloying of the living *subjective* matter with non-living *objective* matter extends far below the ken of the microscope, and that the finest food particles, even after they are drawn into the nucleus of a cell and have apparently become incorporated into the living matter as a part of the protoplasmic substance, are yet sometimes far from being wholly transformed into the living condition. We conceive, indeed, that the purest terrestrial protoplasm, if subjected to a vastly higher power of amplification, would present to our vision an intrinsically dissimilar and often incongruous mass, made up of tracts and streams of actually living matter, really *subjective* and altogether sentient, mingled with *lumps* and unregenerate tracts of matter, still retaining the structure of the formed matter of other organisms from which it had been taken to serve as food.

In the gray matter of the brain, we doubt not, would be found the purest protoplasm, that least alloyed with adventitious substances. To what depths of the atomicity of matter this condition of the alloy of the *subjective* by the *objective* extends, it would be vain to conjecture. Very far, it is quite likely, for even the imagination finds difficulty in picturing the purely subjective living condition of matter as separable from the objective non-living and gross condition under which the bulk of all matter outside that within our own individual quota presents itself to our personal perception.

At the risk of iteration, the terms *objective* and *subjective* matter, as herein used in relation to living matter and its attribute of free will, may again be defined a little more fully. By the subjective matter of a living organism is meant the living matter in the cells, joined together by cell filaments and the nervous system, and constituting that co-sentient substance in which the self-conscious personality appears. In a word, living matter, so fully and sentiently united, that it constitutes a self-mass, to the perception of which all other matter in the world appears to be *not self*, *but something outside of self.*

In separate, unicellular life, the entire world is objective matter to each cell — or nucleus of a cell — representing an infusorial creature and constituting an individual life.

In inorganic matter, too, the entire world may be objective to every separate particle or "atom."

But the consentient relationship of particle to particle, in protoplasm, enables a million particles to unite in a cell, as a *self*, and band together in regarding all save their own company as objective and external.

In pluricellular creatures, where millions of cells are associated in animal tissues, and cell is linked to cell by living protoplasmic filaments, a larger *self* is possible, including, albeit somewhat less perfectly, all those millions of smaller selves in one larger, stronger personality to which the world outside is, in turn, objective.

Protoplasm, then, is that blending or relationship of material particles which permits of the growth of personality, from the lowly self-sentience of a material particle up to that of a human intellect.

The subjective living matter of the human organism is that which is so closely combined in the co-sentient state, that it establishes a limit about itself and sets a boundary mark between self and non-self, and which is able to look out from the citadel of self-hood upon all the rest of the universe, as upon something external and objective. Subjective living matter is that which is on the self side of personal perception and feeling; the personal side of the boundary between sentience and that which sentience passes into when, transformed to will power, it compasses the movement of objective or outer matter; or in other words, when it passes out of the static sentient condition *into effect*.

Such a *modicum* of subjective living matter is subjective, even as it is self-conscious, *only to itself;* to the perception of all other living creatures, it is as objective as is a stone.

The most perfect example of such subjectivity would perhaps be the smallest possible particle, or " atom" of matter, *in its consciousness of itself*. But in the connected protoplasm of an animal organism there is possible, from its co-sentient relationship, a quantitative increase and a projection of self-hood from one particle to many.

A cell appears to have been the largest coherent mass of living matter into which self-hood at first extended, in early terrestrial life.

The various tissues of the animal organism also possess a species of personality, not all of which is surrendered into the personality of the brain tissue. Every separate cell of the tissues, too, retains to a considerable degree its tiny personality. But the nerve and brain tissue, from its coherence and close relation, cell to cell, forms

a practically complete and well rounded personality ; a
mass of living matter, over which the subjective cordon
of selfdom is powerfully projected.   In the brain and
nerves there is so continuous a connection of the living
gray matter by means of filaments from cell to cell, that
the whole forms a practically unified mass in which the
subjective self-conscious state prevails.   It is the coherent, living, gray mass which, so far as it is purely
living matter, constitutes the intellect.   To this portion
of the organism all the rest of the world is objective.

The mere avoirdupois of the subject will portray to
any thinker why it is that quite a portion of the body
of a person appears to his intellect to be of the nature
of external matter and objective.   In a hundred and
fifty pounds' weight — that of an average human organism — there is from fifteen to twenty pounds, according
to the age, of what we term protoplasm.   Of this about
four pounds may be classed as the tissue of intellect ;
but it is not likely that more than a single pound of it
is actually *pure* living matter : protoplasm, unalloyed
by "formed matter" and inorganic matter, and in the
coherent, consentient state of personality.

All the rest is more or less in the condition of objec-
tivity, and external to the self-consciousness ; and in
this, indeed, biology but demonstrates the testimony of
our common sense which constantly gives the impression that our bodies are in part of non-living matter,
not strictly of the nature of our consentient, self-conscious part ; but that there is yet within us a part which
is living and self-conscious ; that which thinks, which
perceives, and which can *will* effects in external objective matter.

The gravest biological question which has come into

prominence within the last decade — not without able adherents on both sides — is that of the interaction of consciousness with motion in protoplasm.

By consciousness I here mean to include self-consciousness; for all consciousness is self-consciousness in less or greater degree.

It has been held that self-consciousness or intelligence is an incidental and passive accompaniment of protoplasmic life, incapable of influencing it; in a word, that the intellect is but a chip on the wave of protoplasmic life; a something which superadds itself to organized living matter, from an independent and unknown source. It follows, of course, from such an hypothesis that there is no such thing as *free* will in living matter; that subjective matter has no real power over objective matter; and that intellect is but a fly on the wheel of evolution.

Several very fanciful definitions of the intellect and the " soul " have of late sprung from this hypothesis; definitions which are highly unsatisfactory, because they reduce what we all actually mean by the terms intellect and soul to something so ethereal, unsubstantial, and uninteresting from a personal point of view, as to make the fate of it before or after death a matter of indifference.

This hypothesis has found admission to the consideration of reputable biologists only from the difficulty experienced in tracing self-consciousness into *will* and will into motion of objective matter.   It became evident that the former theory of a *direct* passage of volition into chemism was an error; and this hypothesis of a disjunct self-consciousness is the transient expression of a doubt whether there is any such interaction as previously claimed.

During the past year the present writer has made an extended study of intracellular hunger and the nature of nutritive energy,— the results of which may, perhaps, be presented hereafter.   One result of these studies, at least, has been to convince me that there is an esoteric plane of matter below chemism, where self-perception is able to cumulate in volition and inaugurate motion. I have no longer a doubt of it, nor that the testimony of our common sense, that we can really *will* effects and accomplish something in the world of matter, is truthful and not a self-deception.

It is evident that, if we could eliminate from the protoplasm of the gray brain all non-living particles of still objective, unregenerate matter and be sure that we had in that gray substance only particles which had entered into the full consentient relationship which constitutes the highest estate and type of living matter, such substance might be properly defined by the word intellect, — *that which knows.*

Define we therefore this quota of purely living matter of the brain as the *intellect:* that part of us which is intelligent, thinks, is self-conscious, remembers, is capable of imagery and can *will* effects out into contiguous matter not included within itself.

The advanced step of thus including within a definition of the word *intellect* the living matter of the brain as well as the sentient constant of that matter, is taken advisedly, and for the reason that matter and its sentient constant are not known to exist separately.   We have no warrant to speak of them as disjoint.

The isolation of the sentient constant of matter is undoubtedly impossible ; — as impossible as the squaring of the circle, the chronometry of eternity, the mensuration of infinity, or the division of 100,000+ by 3 without a remainder.

In this connection, *mind* may be incidentally defined as *the intellect in activity*; and in another sense as the general business of the intellect.

On the whole, the writer can find no good or sufficient authority in the facts of biology for defining the *soul* otherwise than as the intellect, as above set forth.

There have been a thousand fanciful and more or less inadequate definitions of the soul of man by classic philosophers, creed-makers, and more modern metaphysicians. But by the soul is here meant the intellect with retained powers of thought, emotion, and intellectual life, in a word, that which we all personally desire to *save*, or *have saved*, for further life.

Anything less in the way of a definition of the human soul is merely a diversion which will always be unsatisfactory, insufficient.

It is here worthy of remark that the souls, or intellects, of all human beings are, from the biological point of view, very imperfect, that is to say, the living matter of which they are composed is not even approximately *pure* or well blended, cell to cell. As an organ too, the intellectual tissue is structurally imperfect, resembling a house built room after room by the addition of lean-tos, ells, and porches, each an afterthought, rather than an edifice reared upon a well-drafted, pre-existent plan.

It will be apparent from the first step of this inquiry that the latest biological conclusion touching the intellect or soul does not contemplate it as separable from the organism, or capable of emigration from the earth, or of residence in other organisms on earth, or of passage through contiguous objective matter and space; nor yet of disembodied emigration from the earth to distant quarters of the universe. Such a conception of the soul is contrary to all that we know of it from biological investigation and is, we believe, an idea founding on nothing more creditable than Oriental fable and the observation of morbid or abnormal conditions of the human brain. We do not see any reason to believe that it is possible or can ever be possible, under nature, for the intellect or soul to be separated or dis-associated from the organism in which it has been raised up and of which it is a part. We make this statement qualified by the phrase, *under nature;* for we do not here raise the question of a supernatural rescue of the soul from the decaying organism.

Biology regards the human soul as a far-derived and complex result of protoplasmic life. The fabric of it is living matter wrought by all its ancestry since protoplasm first stirred on the earth. Since the earliest metazoic ganglion first served as a little brain, with special senses servant to it, the development of the soul began. It is the formative arrangement of particles and their co-sentient relationship one with another which constitutes intelligence and which is requisite to make the gray living matter *intellect.* In illustration, if an equal mass and weight of bone protoplasm, or muscle protoplasm, or liver protoplasm were put in the place of the gray brain protoplasm, we should not have intellect, or soul, inside the skull, although we might have sentience of low grade. Muscle protoplasm has developed along its line of ancestry with a view and purpose to accomplish contractility and attain a high degree of excellence in this specialty. It is sentient, but in low degree, its internal arrangement and energy having been turned to the task of self-movement lengthwise and breadthwise. It is possible if some unusual change of its conditions of existence should call for the reception of impressions from the external world and the assumption of the function of nerves and brain, that even a cell of muscular protoplasm might, in time, relinquish its office of contractility and, in the course of ages, develop the capacity to receive the data of knowledge and become intelligent. For living matter is wonderfully self-adaptive to its environment and susceptible to the stress of the circumstances by which it is conditioned. But to change the internal arrangement of a muscle cell to that of a brain cell, or to build up the peculiar arrangement of such a brain cell from even a cell of undifferentiated, virgin protoplasm like that which we see in primitive unicellular life, would no doubt require a time period at which even a paleontologist would heave a sigh.

For were such a cell of living matter magnified till it should equal the earth in apparent size, the particles, such as we know it to be composed of, would still be no larger than grains of sand; and in its complex and delicate arrangement, we conceive that a cell of the gray brain would call for the exact and elaborate grouping of all these particles, one with another, in a particular manner and at particular distances apart; and that, still further, these groups of particles would be arranged in well-nigh infinite patterns, standing for the mnemonic tracery of color, sound, and sense — equal in intricacy to the arrangement of the single letters and words of a vast library of books, piled tier on tier upon a thousand shelves.   This picture, indeed, would fall pigmy-short of the real facts.

As a factor of the intellect and soul we must involve ancestral effects in the brain substance from an experience of life through time which is only subtended by the epochs of geology.   Time and experience of the living matter have entered as formal factors into the human soul and could not be withdrawn from it without a reduction of the co-sentient relationship of the soul substance ; a reduction, descending to the low, early sentience of primordial protoplasm.

It is upon this elaborate fabric wrought in the protoplasm of intellect, that intelligence depends, and without which the intellect or soul would be no longer rational, or intellectual.

Disorganized, the particles of the gray brain matter would not be destroyed, indeed, and would be at once available for use in other protoplasm, yet would be no better for such use than any other particles ; for they would retain each only its primordial sentient constant ; since the relationship and arrangement in which they stood in the brain cells alone represented knowledge and intelligence.

The dissolution of the brain substance as surely presages the dissolution of intelligence and the cessation of mind, as the taking to pieces of a clock and the smelting of the metal wheels, argues the cessation of its function as a time-recording apparatus.   In the one case the metal in a homogeneous mass would remain, but not a clock ; in the other, the homogeneously sentient matter would remain, but not an intellect, in the sense in which alone a person's soul is valuable to him, or worth preservation.

Such a conclusion may dissipate certain fond and long-indoctrinated illusions, yet none the less the real fact and the truth should always be sought and, when perceived, adhered to. For in all the universe there is no such precious pearl as truth. Truth — despite all the specious reasonings of some modern pessimists·and bad philosophers — is always healthful to life ; and its discovery tends to the achievement of immortal life.

When from the subjective side, we attempt to take cognizance of our personality, by introspection of its phenonena, the results of our self-search confirm this conclusion.

For example, when we self-consciously think, there is first sentience, or perception of the impressions previously received (memory) in the large multipolar cells beneath the cortex of the brain, and we are at the same time conscious of an intellectual effort — which effort is the intercommunication of hundreds and thousands of these cells, each an individual self, in which are stored the experience of the outer world, obtained through the special and general senses. This experience is garnered there as the form of objects seen, sounds heard, contacts felt and, in general, all manner of experiences, simple and complex. This wonderful capacity for form also includes opinions and conclusions arrived at by previous thinking. Our personal perception represents all this to us as something pictured and based on form and figure, representing dimensions and material symbolism ; in a word, something dependent on an arrangement of the material component substance, or living matter, in relationship, particle to particle. We are subjectively conscious, too, that but for this *form* and relationship we should be without the *data* for thought and should possess sentience only. Memory implies form and arrangement in the cell contents, and thinking founds on a sentient interchange of individual memory, cell with cell, and different special tracts of cells one with another.

Thus it is that knowledge depends on experience. But for experience the brain would be merely sentient, incapable of intelligent thought, or reason, or memory. When we speak of the intellect or soul, we mean the organized, formed, *experienced* living substance of the brain cells, not their sentient capacity only.

Pluricellular man : Whence is his soul?

Let him who knows whence came matter with its sentient constant, answer.

On the vast breadth of Void has appeared a mystery which men now call *Matter*, but whose real name, like that of Rome, no tongue may utter.

What is the soul?

It is the developed and *experienced* living matter of the body, particularly that in the cells of the nerve ganglia and of the brain *par excellence*. Self-consciousness and personality are not located exclusively in any one cell of living matter, or tract of such cells, but in the whole continent mass, although it is manifest that it is centralized and largely, very largely, located in the brain ; and the development of that organ, as shown by the position, course, and termination of nerve fibres, would indicate that the gray matter of the *corpora striata, thalami* and *corpora quadrigemina* may be its *sedes.*

Too much importance need not be given such localization, however.   The human brain is by no means an ideally developed organ, but resembles rather some antique family mansion which has grown, by frequent annexes and the addition of ells and gables, through many generations. The point of real importance is, that every cell of it contains not only the data of memory and life experience, but these data set down in a sentient substance, sentiently recorded and arranged, every particle of which substance goes to swell the organic self-consciousness. Personality, or self-consciousness, must not be dissociated from these mnemonic data and portrayed as a something distinct from them. These data in the cells, the results of life experience, *are themselves self-conscious.*

Given present, matter, elementally sentient, the soul of pluricellular man is the consentient living matter (cells) of his intellectual tissue, developed and continent of the results of development, since protoplasm first appeared on the earth.

Take from this definition any constituent, and from the "soul" of man which it describes, some necessary attribute will be found wanting.

Let not this definition of the soul be misunderstood, nor judged according to the old formula of theological criticism.

Not matter inert, insentient, is soul,— there is no such matter in the world, — but matter, the universal embodiment of power, life, and intelligence ; the sentient, cosmic proteus, the archeus of nature ; matter which holds the initial elements of life and tends to develop human and divine intelligence in the ascending orders of terrestrial life ; matter which under favorable con-

ditions will approximate omniscience and attain omnipotence ; matter which as we know it on earth,
elementally sentient only, may yet have developed
divinely on elder orbs of cosmos, not once but a thousand times, across the wide reaches of the eternal past,
and have within its scheme unnumbered developments
in the eternal future.

Every religious system of mankind which has included
philosophy and culture has in the end developed an
equivalent conception. Brahma broods self-contempla-
tive, alternately diffusing himself abroad and re-deifying
his powers. Jehovah and God, in the slow refinements
of Christian theology, are already taking on the form
and lineaments of Brahma.

V.

WHAT BECOMES OF THE SOUL?

WITHIN the last decade, biological researches have shed a flood of light on this long mysterious question of the fate of man after death.   Discovery, in the field of *living matter*, has added fact to fact till we have what may fairly be termed a *science of living matter*, which embraces much certain knowledge on subjects hitherto obscure.   It is indeed as if a powerful beam of electric light were projected into some musty subterranean chamber, some dank old tomb of Pharaohs, the haunt of ghostly superstitions, noisome with legends still half believed, of Styx and hells, and fulsome with too dulcet promises of paradise; a strange, abnormal nether world of fancy and fantasy, long in need of the wholesome light of day.

Into this old kingdom of shades our science has shot its beam, and lo! as when at dawn the ghosts and bats and ravening things of night slink away and vanish, so here old fables, spookism, and all the sacerdotal phantasmagoria of eld fade out suddenly; and the actual facts are seen to be quite simple.

Something of poetry and certain too fond dreams of post-mortal Nirvanas are undoubtedly dissipated by the keen bright light and the in-rush of fresh air.   Many whose minds have long fed on legend and faith will experience a certain sadness and sinking of hope, as the truth is seen to be different from old creeds.

It could not be otherwise. The actual facts of life are never so fine as those mirages of our longings, which it is the mission of science to disperse; and some there are who will still prefer illusion to fact, so be that they can derive a little more present comfort. Only a few, however. The good hard sense of a majority of mankind will always prefer fact to self-deception.

And here, too, as in many another instance, where olden error has given place to younger truth, after the first sense of loss and disappointment is past, the facts will be seen to form the basis and the earnest of a better faith, broader, more ennobling, which during the next century will possess mankind, presenting loftier ideals, prompting to purer endeavor and greater achievement. Already such a faith is in the world. Its stern, new gospel sets forth a scheme of moral and physical regeneration, such as has never been taught before. It contemplates the complete control by man of the energies of nature, the paradisation of the earth and the prolongation of life.

With a general reference to the theory and definition given of the human intellect, or soul, in the preceding paper, the psychic question of this one may be answered in no uncertain terms.

In universal matter we behold a substance at once objective and subjective in a manner at present inexplicable to human intelligence. It consists of particles; whether divisible infinitely or ultimately indivisible is not yet known. This is known, however: the particles of matter as small as the quadrillionth of a grain in weight possess each a certain property or quota of energy which is never known to vary in tension or be separated from it. In whatever relation to other particles this specified particle may enter, through all the multitudinous combinations, actions, and reactions of terrestrial and cosmic chemism, it always evinces and can never be robbed or in any way deprived of this its natural endowment of energy. In fact, the constancy of gravitation, the coefficient of electro-magnetic activity, the entire economy of heat, light, and world formation, — in a word, the stability and *rationale* of the whole visible universe of suns and worlds rests and depends on the unvarying attribute or property of the particle.

Streams of these particles enter the cell of life constantly, assume while in it a certain peculiar relationship one to another, and while in this relationship, the group or cell thus formed *feels*, *lives*, or, in other words, exhibits the *subjective side* of matter. As a result of this self-consciousness the cell contents exhibits *individuality*; *i. e.*, acts and behaves like an independent little world within the greater world. Even as the universe evinces personality on a vast scale, the cell of terrestrial life shows individuality on a small scale. The universe displays a certain grand personality which mankind has always been inclined to deify in one way or another, although there is little reason to think — every reason, indeed, not to think — it of a high order of intelligence, but rather of low sentience.

As the universe of matter pursues its courses and acts from a manifest inward impulsion of sentient selfhood, even so the little cell of living matter is seen to move this way and that about its personal business, a tiny reduplication of the all-inclosing macrocosm.

The material particles departing from the cell and dropping out of the protoplasmic relationship, are seen to have *lost* no iota of their original energy. Again, after a few hours or days, they may re-enter and become a constituent part of the same cell, perhaps, again exhibiting the same ability to feel and live there, ere long to depart as before.

From these data the conclusion has been derived that, underlying the quota of energy constantly exhibited by every particle there is a static sentient property which we have termed the sentient-constant, or subjective component, of universal matter; for the universe of matter exhibits a self-actuating power which can arise only from a sentient or subjective property. In like manner the protoplasmic cell evinces a self-directive power which we know to be the result of sentience.

Hence the theorem of this treatise, namely, that matter is at bottom sentient matter and the universe a *living*, self-moving universe, there being on an esoteric and profound plane of the former, a passage of sentience into motion.

We hold this position to be logically impregnable on any other ground than that there is in cosmos an alien force not of it, but injected into it, from some point outside it; and there is nothing in nature as we know it which requires such an hypothesis to explain phenomena. Such an hypothesis, moreover, can be shown to be immoral.

The particles of matter — divisible still, or finally indivisible — are hence of the nature of sentient units and the prototypes of immortality in the universe, since they present themselves as synonymes of the indestructible and the eternal.

Of such sentient units the intellect or soul of man is a temporary aggregation possessing the elements, indeed, of immortal life, but ephemeral as yet by reason of the vicissitudes and destructive influences of the crude, rough, tumultuous *habitat* in which it lives.

The soul, literally speaking, is or contains part and parcel of a quantity of living matter or protoplasm, which began life on the earth's surface one hundred millions of years ago, as it is likely,— literally a part of that identical protoplasm which alternately, as a germ or fertilized *ovum*, expands by growth into an organism and recedes into a germ.

Carried away by this view, certain biologists have even defined the soul of man as this deathless "germ-plasm," and pictured it as realizing the immortality to which the human intellect aspires. But which one of us would be long satisfied with such an immortality as that?—the survival of an *ovum!* It requires but a moment of clear reflection to see that it is only in the full grown brain and nerve ganglia that personality rises to the proportions of the soul, that soul which we so ardently desire to secure " salvation " for. It is the intellectual tissue of the organism at its best and fullest growth which constitutes the soul, not the impersonal little germ of a human life, seen in the reproductive elements. The germ is but a very limited, imperfect method of immortal life, a little better than extinction but attended by the utter loss of memory and personality. Moreover, as can be shown, the germ form of survival is a mode or condition resulting from stress of a hard theatre of life. The only condition or estate of the human soul really worth saving, from the individual or personal point of view, is the full-grown organic estate, and that alas! still perishes with the organism.

The sentient particles of matter, indeed, survive and

enter other organisms, but personality, memory, and general intelligence are dissolved and lost; and it is personality and memory which of all things we are most anxious to save. No form or promise of immortality which omits personality and memory can ever be grateful or satisfactory to man. The human aspiration is ever toward fuller personality, clearer memory, and greater intelligence than experienced in the present limited life-time.

What becomes of the soul?

First, what becomes of the soul during life?

In attempting to give an answer direct to this latter question, it will be necessary to reopen a discussion briefly alluded to in the preceding paper.

Owing to the difficulties at present attending a demonstration of the interaction of sentience with motion, there has arisen a new sect of fatalists in biological science, who assume that sentience and self-consciousness in the cell, do not interact to produce movement, but are adventitious phenomena — an apparition appearing there from another sphere, between which and motion there is no correlation, no interaction. Sentience and self-consciousness — according to this theory — appear in the brain as an incidental sequence, but have no power to influence protoplasmic activity there; and intelligence is, therefore, *a mysterious something from somewhere* which descends or ascends and alights on protoplasm.

This hypothesis is gratuitous. Its only *raison d'être* is the fact that the correlation between sentience and motion is not yet fully der nstrated. It is, in short, an argument of the famous " missing link " variety. "Find the missing link," exclaimed, for years, the opponents of evolution; " you have not found it, hence there is no evolution."

Certain adherents of this theory of incidental sentience in nature have, of late, tripped very innocently in their ratiocination, putting forward the doctrine that while man can do nothing personally by self-effort of his intellect, the human race may be *improved* by a matching-off of one physical law against another! The fact that this act of matching-off implies an effect of intelligence in physics, appears to have been quite lost sight of.

If self-consciousness is an adventitious incident in nature, then, indeed, does fate prevail and every pessimist is a wise man. There is no " free will " in living matter; and nature, whether benignly devised, or a " devil's game at skittles," will run its course uninfluenced and unimproved by human effort. In a word, the theory is immoral and the *distemper* of its immorality will be felt by any one who attempts to think it out to its logical conclusion. It resembles many another theory of closet philosophers, so very many of which are contributed to modern philosophy, profound after a manner, yet murky, presenting some phase of truth with elaborate patience, yet failing to open the question up from top to bottom in a clear light. All such have first to be corrected for aberration and bad relativity.

If the sentient hypothesis of matter and of the universe is correct, if free will in living matter is not the most cruel of delusions, if humanity has any power to advance itself in the world, *then sentience does interact with motion, and self-consciousness is able to will movement in matter*. A fuller demonstration of this great truth will be attempted in the future; here, for the present, it is assumed to be true.

It is not held here, however, that sentience passes by a direct *saltus* into visible motion, any more than would be argued that sunlight passes directly into the motion of the piston of a steam-engine, overlooking the intermediate steps of vegetation, oxidation, and aqueous expansion. So in the case of the interaction of self-consciousness in living matter, with movement outward, there is action on inferior planes of matter, a succession of steps, which we indistinctly perceive, when we think of *willing* an act.

The static sentient constant of the particles of matter is, we conceive, sustained at integrity from the equilibrium of cosmos. Every exercise of the will, every designed direction of self-conscious attention, draws on and expends the sentient property of matter in motion of contiguous particles. For motion in nature is of sentient origin, *subjective* as delivered from one particle to another, *objective* after the impulse is received by the second particle — objective ever afterwards, indeed, till in the cycle of the universe the objective returns to its source. Thus the self-consciousness of the soul is projected outward, by will, into contiguous matter, and man becomes a matter-moving agent in the world.

The bulk of self-consciousness, *i. e.*, the aggregated sentience of the cells of the organism, is expended in *thinking*, in sustaining personality, and maintaining the organism in function.

The cells of the various tissues, the glandular and the muscular, for example, are employed in preparing and storing up chemical substances from which, through a chain of katabolic reductions, locomotion and digestion may be performed, processes to which the organic consciousness has but to give an initial impulse. The personal self-consciousness of every living organism is an agent from which effects or *work* may be derived, and the quantity and quality of this work will be in proportion to the medium furnished it for passing into effect. One person might spend his intellect in thinking merely, and die without leaving any perceptible record of this thought. Another, superadding the muscular contraction of his fingers in forming legible characters, might think the same or similar thoughts and set them in intelligible array before the world, thus vastly influencing his fellows. It is largely a question of the means of transferrence and record. So of the statesman, so of the inventor, the commander, the monarch ; there are thousands who could do as much and as well, or better, than these, but have lacked the means of thus projecting their intellects into effects.

How large a part of this purely personal energy is constantly expended and demanded to sustain the organism in function, or maintain life, has never been exactly determined, and apparently varies in different organisms and at various stages of life ; a large part, nine tenths of it, considered as a matter-moving agency, probably, yet a part is available for work outside the organism. From bodily habit and the conditions of the intra-organic draughts on the intellectual tissue, little heed is taken of these expenditures for the most part ; and in making use of terms so purely dynamic, it seems again necessary to state distinctly that the interaction of consciousness with motion is entirely intracellular, and that in the ordinary visible bodily functions there is never a direct passage of sentience or the subjective state into movement, or objective phenomena.

This interaction takes place on an interior plane of matter within protoplasm proper.

But from the connection of cell with cell by protoplasmic filaments, and the devotion of different tissues or tracts of cells to the production of substances of various degrees of chemical tension, digestion, circulation, and assimilation are accomplished, as also muscular contraction, locomotion, work, and mental processes. None the less, the sentience, more or less developed, within the cell gives the initial, directive impulse. From that inaugural and directive impulse sets off all that man does, all that the race has done on the earth's surface; and in the giving of that impulse, the soul is hourly, daily, and yearly expended, as long as the person lives. Obedient to that impulse, the magazine of chemical and mechanical energy stored up in the organism, may raise a weight of a hundred pounds to the top of a mountain, or slowly lower the same weight down the mountain. It is not that personal intelligence is transformed to the mechanical power which does this work, or is the direct dynamic equivalent of it, but that it goes into a directive impulse which determines *when*, *how*, and *to what purpose* the organic energy shall be expended.

The elemental sentience of a number of tons of matter contributes to the soul of a human being during its seventy or eighty years of life. The character or plan of that life as uttered by the organism, is, even during life, gradually marred and obliterated. The clear perception of pleasure and pain, of truth and error is, in the vast majority of persons, slowly dimmed and destroyed, owing to the "aging" of the organism. But although the personality of such a soul is outworn and approaching dissolution, the work which it has inaugurated in contiguous matter remains a more or less enduring result of its life. In a certain sense, the soul survives in this work. This is of itself a species of immortality, but not that boon of life which we so earnestly long for.

To trace the continuous expenditure of the human intellect for any given time, a minute, an hour, or a year, is one of the most interesting of investigations. It is this expenditure of intelligence which underlies the entire progressive development of organisms on the earth.

To develop the human body and the tissue of intellect, the intelligences of a long series of animal orders have been expended through vast time periods. The "souls" of these older animal orders were all put forth to make progress in organisms. We exist by virtue of that long expenditure. For the fierce struggles amidst the reeds of those old marsh continents we are the stronger and wiser to-day. Not only have our human sires fought for us the wars of political and moral liberty, but the brutes as well. An infinite tenderness and pity fills the heart of the true naturalist as he pores on their long mouldering bones. They have lived and laid down their lives for us. Nay, they have yielded their very souls to us. Their souls were spent to equip the human organism and are, in a sense, pent in it still, even as the olden sunshine is imprisoned in the coal measures. The capacity for mind in the body and brain of man exists and is bequeathed only at the expense of the soul of ancestral life.

It is not alone in books that the effects of intellectual life are preserved. In every nation or community

of man there is always an ever-growing accumulation
of those effects which descend from generation to generation, *orally*, in maxims, adages, trades, crafts, and
traditions. The course and manner of human life is
directed in great part by these consolidated experiences
of intellect in the past. To secure the proof of truth
contained in each of such maxims and to verify each
detail of a craft, soul has been expended and thus
passed into effect.

The human organism must be regarded as built up on
a definite plan which exists actually or potentially in
the embryo, and which has been perfecting itself ever
since the simplest organisms swam in earth's primitive
seas. Although constantly copied and continuously
renewed, the body of man is yet one of the oldest
things on earth, older than the granitic mountains, older
perhaps than the present continents.

The organism of man is thus the resultant of a
world-long struggle for a means of intelligent expression by the elemental sentience. Nature labors to
bring forth omniscience and omnipotence. The human soul comes into existence by virtue of an organic
process which it has been the object of the best effort
of terrestrial life to bring to its present state of excellence : so costly and so holy a thing is the body of
man. It is the accumulated inheritance of the ages.

Our libraries are reservoirs of soul effects, or preserved intellectual life. The graphic conservation of
intelligence has thus become a most efficient aid to
assist posterity. Instead of being dissipated in irre-
claimable effects, experience is held in store. The
effect of the soul of a Newton and a Faraday is found
in their recorded discoveries ; and although they no

longer continue to live, their expended and recorded souls still instruct us. In books they have attained a personally insentient immortality; the effect of their souls has been *saved*.

Wealth, treasure, even money may, in a sense, be regarded as an amassed store of soul, an hereditament acquired from the expenditure of intelligence in the past.

What becomes of the soul at death?

To those who, jealous for creed's sake, sometimes criticise in the inquisitorial spirit, it is distinctly stated at the outset that this paper does not treat, either *pro* or *con*, unless inferentially, of the salvation or condemnation of the " soul " of man or beast, at the hands of supernatural beings. Faith in the interposition of a pitying or avenging deity, outside of nature, is not here discussed. Concerning such tenets the only position taken is that such salvation or condemnation of a soul, disembodied and separated from matter, would be an essentially supernatural and miraculous act; and that from the very nature of things such tenets must ever remain a matter of " faith," without evidence. The purpose here is to set forth, not what may be done for man by an agency outside nature, but what man may do for himself under nature.

The entire vast literature of the soul and its fortunes after death founds on a definition of soul of which biological science has no knowledge: a definition utterly unlike what all present knowledge of nature and of matter would lead us to give.

All theories of spiritism and the " disembodied " soul rest, in reality, on the assumption that " force "or energy in nature is separable from matter and may exist apart from it; whereas, so far as science can determine, there is no such thing in nature, or in cosmos, as *pure* force. Disassociated from energy, too, matter would no longer be matter to the senses. We could not have knowledge of it; and there is no reason to believe that the two components ever exist separate, or are separable. For this reason belief in "disembodied souls" must always remain a matter of *faith* merely, and fall within the category of the supernatural. Science can never obtain knowledge of the supernatural; and to the present writer it appears of *the nature of a physical impossibility that such knowledge can be received through any of the senses or modes of perception possessed by man.*

The biological answer to the question, whether the human soul is immortal under nature, depends wholly on what is meant by the word *soul*. And it is here that the minds of most persons become bewildered, and hence tend to disagreement.

If by *soul* is meant the elemental sentience of the matter which forms the intellectual tissue, then the soul of man is immortal,— as immortal as the universe itself. The particles of living matter are indestructible and never part with their primary energy. Nothing either of substance or elemental sentience which goes to make up soul is ever destroyed by death or ceases to exist in cosmos.

If by soul is meant the effect produced by the expenditure of the personal intelligence on other human beings and on the world at large, that effect, or work done, does not cease at the death of the person; it remains a factor for good or ill through all time, even after the name and individuality of the dead person are forgotten by all the living.

If by soul is meant that veritable part of the human living protoplasm which descends from parent to offspring in the embryo, bearing ancestral traits, characteristics and the race stamp, — all those directive and formative tendencies which make the human embryo grow to be man or woman, instead of a tree, a dog, or an ox, — then indeed does the human soul survive in children and has survived through the long eras of evolution, since the primary racial protoplasm first came into being. It will live as long as the race lives.

If by soul is meant all which the intellectual tissue or living matter is and contains from inheritance, in a word, personality, imagination, memory, ambition, the *ego*, capable of *willing* effects and subject to pain and pleasure, hope and fear, then the certainty that it ceases to exist under nature at organic death is so complete, that belief in its disembodied survival is a mere fantasy.

And this is one of those hard truths of our century and our sciences which display at first sight a grim and relentless aspect, but are necessarily disclosed to drive us forward to invention and achievement.

VI.

IS IT POSSIBLE TO SAVE THE SOUL?

SUCH is the present stage and estate of the evolution of life on the earth, from the biological point of view; such the human situation.

Frankly, the writer would not have deemed it worth the while to prepare these papers if he believed there were no further word to be spoken.

If I saw nothing more in evolution than humanity always dying and ever doomed to death, I would not add a further page to the iteration of its death sentence.

There are those who think differently, however.

Of late, within the last five years, a new school of philosophy has arisen among us, a school which I believe to be utterly defective in its conclusion, the more defective the more detrimental to truth, in that its premises are well chosen.

For it founds broadly and well in the monistic conception of the universe. Its working motive is meliorism, or the betterment of mankind. It recognizes the fact, that the soul — meaning thereby, personality, memory, self-consciousness — cannot exist apart from the organism, and defines individual man as a transitory embodiment of the soul of humanity.

Thence, devoid of faith, it concludes that with thirty, fifty, or a hundred years of life, man as an individual must rest content, although the effects of his life, or soul, survive in the life of the race ; and in his offspring, a germinal portion of his living substance which does not, however, transmit self-consciousness, survives and may survive indefinitely. Hence we are advised to sink our personality in the grander life of humanity; to merge our self interests in those of the race.

Death, organic and personal death, it is held, is the common lot and law of nature. Nowhere is there any hope of escape. Death is the necessary end of life; in the future as in the past man will live only to die.

Thus does a school of scientific philosophy apply, wrongfully apply, the present facts of biology to morals and religion.

A religion it may become, but at best it would be a religion of despair, relieved only by periodical outbursts of pessimism. The great, warm, hopeful heart of humanity could never accept it. A faith it can hardly become; for there is not the element of *faith* or hope in it.

Alluding to the reluctance of the German people to accept this negative doctrine concerning immortality, frank, out-spoken Hæckel petulantly remarks, " but the mass of mankind want above all things their personal *ego* immortality, and everything else stands in second rank."

True, wholly true, and based on a deeper-lying biological truth than has yet been recognized.

Monism, meliorism, *and resignation to death as the necessary and natural end of human personality and intellect!* And is this, then, the outcome of the heroic struggle of evolution?

Most men, doomed to death, are brave enough to meet it with a certain firmness and sometimes with reckless gayety. None the less, such is not a normal condition of mind or heart.

Philosophers who have philosophized their brains to a condition of world-weariness, and educated, elderly persons who have fortified their minds with the tenets of the above weary philosophers, may accept such a creed without very poignant regret.

The young and normal will shrink from it with a shudder; and the uneducated will never accept it, so long as a ritual is preached which presents a promise of more life.

The error of this conclusion touching human life is deep in its premises. This philosophy grasps not the true and real principle of life and soul. It rejects personality and makes little of individual man. It has failed to comprehend the fact, *that life never exists save as self.* It confounds personality with impersonality, and calmly asks the personal to become impersonal, to blot itself out.

Let us here iterate two principles of life, set forth in a preceding paper.

The point to be particularly emphasized, the truth without recognition of which no correct or adequate conception of the human soul can be formed, is that the *root of personality* is in the cell. In the cell a certain *circle* of sentience— the elemental sentience of particles —is formed, the *axis of which is self*, self-conscious-ness, personality. In the brain many thousand cells are joined by filaments of living matter in such sentient union that they all blend together in a personal one, or *ego;* but the root and origin of it all is in the personal self of the cell.

When this fact is lost sight of, or given less than its full recognition, the true conception of the human intel-lect is vitiated and goes astray. The cell is ever what the individual citizen is to the nation, the essential living unit.

From this fact, which may be ranked as the first principle of psychology, we pass to the second, also of primary significance.

A unicellular creature, or a cell of a pluricellular animal, exhibits self, or personality, in proportion to the quality, age, health, and general well-being of the *modicum* of living matter contained therein. In other words, the strength of self, or personality, depends on the health and activity of the protoplasm of the cell. Self-consciousness slackens in vividness and power as the living matter of the cell deteriorates, becomes restricted by "formed matter," or starved for lack of food particles. Whatever agency, indeed, depresses the protoplasmic activity of the cell, diminishes self-hood at its axial origin in exact proportion. This self-hood is the origin of individual life. Life slackens as the personality slackens ; and death is but the total cessation of self-hood. A cell lives only as it utters self.

In young full normal health, its personality is strong. In disease and that consummation of noxious and restrictive agencies which we term old age, personality is weak, and weakens to its cessation. Self or personality always resists all agencies which tend to weaken or end it.

It is as if the component, elementally sentient particles formed a certain pyrrhic circle or sphere about the cell's axis, and that the subjective self or personality arose from it. Whatever breaks this pyrrhic union of the particles, breaks self, destroys personality. Self appears from the concatenation of life-abounding particles, as the iris shines from the lighted rain-drops, and ceases when sunshine and rain-drops cease to interact; and hence certain of our modern philosophers have been led to regard self and personality as an *incident* merely of cell life. But this is a partial view, leading to grave error. The cell never really becomes a cell, till subjective self *reacts* in it, by the, as yet, little-demonstrated steps of will-power. Otherwise, there would be no *free will* in the world; and an insentient fatalism would prevail throughout the universe. But one intelligent glance down the tube of the microscope, at the humblest little bacterium will show that his subjective self is in reaction there on the external world; in a word that he is *self-controlled*. A cell is a self. A unicellular creature is a single self. A pluricellular creature is an *e-pluribus-unum* of cell selves, so connected by living bonds of the self-same protoplasm, that they can express all their selves as one. None the less, the seat of all self-consciousness, feeling, pleasure, and pain is in the cell, and there inheres and remains, not only in unicellular creatures, but in pluricellular quite as fixedly.

Hence it is for the cells that our solicitude should extend. Our care must ever be for these. Self and subjectivity reside there and there only; and life is strong only as self is vividly exhibited.

These are biological facts, and their bearing on the present question is apparent.

The philosophy which counsels resignation to death, the sinking of self in humanity, the merging of personality in the life of the race, is a philosophy of self-obliteration, a doctrine of death. The reception of such ideas and their adoption into daily thought and practice, cannot be otherwise than obstructive to human life. The passivity and apathy of certain Oriental peoples, are, in part, due to the long prevalence of similar doctrines. The progress and *élan* of Western peoples comes measurably from the prominent exhibition of self and the culture of *personality* in individual men.

Remarkable men the world over have always displayed strong self and even aggressive personality. Self (not a futile "selfishness") is to be cultivated in every human being; and humanity will never be strong till it is composed of personally strong men and women, not resigned to die and sink their souls in an abstraction, but determined to live and secure for themselves omnipotence and immortality.

For what is humanity, this humanity in which we are advised to sink our personality and merge our souls? This humanity which "wants above all things its personal *ego* immortality, and holds all else in second rank"? What is it but a million or a billion of personalities? Will any one be so obtuse as to define humanity as the ova, or germs, by means of which one personality now makes shift to bring another into existence? Will any one hold that we ought in moral obligation to stop living, in order that these little make-shifts of life may continue to come into existence *per se?* Is not the race-life a herd of individual lives? Does it suffer or take pleasure otherwise than in these individual lives?

It is the welfare of the individual which is to be considered, not humanity or the race; for humanity, otherwise than as individuals, is an abstraction. When we speak of working for the race and of self-sacrifice for humanity's sake, we mean for the sake of a certain

number of individuals. Heredity, inherited excellences,
transmitted traits, are of no value till they appear
in individuals. It is not the germ plasm of mankind
that constitutes the *raison d'être* of life, but the adult
man and woman. It should be our care to save persons, not germs. Germs are of consequence only because adults cannot yet be preserved.

The school of scientific philosophy that accepts death
as a finality of personal life neither grasps the real
significance of evolution, nor has any true conception
of the promise in terrestrial life. Even the best of our
scientific men seem to experience great difficulty in
shaking off the idea that human beings must *always die*
because, forsooth, they have died thus far. But the
dream of all the ages of mankind is immortal life, not
for the race, but for the individual. The existent faith
in disembodied soul life after bodily death is but the
mirage of souls thirsty for deathless life ; a fantasy, but
a glorious one — one in keeping with the spirit and
genius of humanity and one that will never be given up
till science has something better to offer men than the
certainty of personal death.

But it has something better. A new conception of
the mission of science is entering the minds of men.
We shall not always die. Personality with its treasures of experience, memory, soul, will not always be
lost after a few years of inexperience and unsuccessful
struggle to live.

The defect, the condemning defect, of this late
school of philosophers, is their failure to grasp the real
significance of the evolution of human life. *Death*
forms a part of their scheme. They see in evolution
only the nether segment of evolution ; its grand arc

which spans the heavens, its promise of deathlessness to living beings, is still unseen.   They bring from their biological studies no tidings to men but the certainty of personal death, and ask them to find their immortality in the germ plasm.   Their creed is a half truth, the dark half.   Such a half truth is as futile as error, and may be even more pernicious.

Monism, meliorism, and a cultivated resignation to death as the best event that can occur, after a life spent in acquiring experience, learning, and all the data suitable and necessary to live !

Monism — a primary truth of nature.

Meliorism — a pleasant and correct doctrine.

Resignation to personal death — a fallacious deduction, a stultification of nature and life.

Life and death are intrinsically antagonistic.   Resignation to personal death there should never be in the sense of acquiescence from principle.   When death is seen to be unavoidable by any exercise of our powers to escape, it is befitting that a decent calmness and fortitude should be summoned to meet it.   But never resignation.   Day or night we should cease not to lament that we must still die on account of the imperfection of our resources and the crude state of our sciences.

Man has developed to live, not to die ; and that is a vain philosophy that builds on death, and a false religion that raises a shrine to it.

Life, longer life, and still more life should be the hope and the faith of humanity.   .

Our sciences will bring prolonged life.   There is in man, moreover, a tissue, the intellectual tissue, which is still progressive in the sense of evolving a new type ; a tissue which will develop deathless life.   Die, we of the present century may and probably shall. We are still too ignorant to attain prolonged life. But there should be no mistake in our mental attitude regarding death. It is ever an untimely fate, the penalty of still imperfect powers and an evil to be retrieved with all our powers ; and even this radical change in our mental attitude touching death, will effect much to intensify and prolong life. In fact, it is the first step toward more life.

One of the most noxious of popular doctrines is that which portrays the human race as having already reached the acme of possible earthly life — as being the best that can be done on the earth in the line of vital evolution. Whereas all the probabilities are that mankind is one of the incipient developments of that evolution. Human beings die on account of the still unreclaimed, unsubjugated conditions of the earth's surface as a *habitat* — not that death is a necessary sequence to life.

The plain truth of the matter appears to be that we do not personally survive death because we are not yet fit to survive. We are not yet worthy of the immortal life, or the prolonged life which we crave. We are still too imperfect for it, intellectually as well as organically. Judged by nature's standard our souls are not yet worth preservation. It is quite as certain, too, that we shall live longer — even become practically immortal — as soon as by earnest research, self effort and endeavor to improve ourselves and our conditions, we have become worthy of it. The universe with all its unlimited opportunities and treasures is before us — to conquer, to possess, to enjoy. Nature neither frowns untowardly, nor yet gratuitously assists us, but yields to our labors with a certain grand, calm pas-

sivity, and seems never to grudge us our well-earned
conquests. It is ours to take and hold. Otherwise,
Nature is not providential. The wall falls and crushes
us, if we do not take care. The fire which we have kin-
dled consumes us, if we do not guard it. There is no
favoritism. With a wide but impartial smile, the great
unconscious objective would seem to say, — Go on if
you desire. I neither let, nor hinder.

To deify nature and look for "providential" care
from her, is to do nature an injustice. The vast do-
main of inorganic matter about us is but elementally
sentient, neither beneficent, nor malevolent. It is a
free and an open field in which we must stand or fall
for ourselves.

These, indeed, may not be tidings with which to
flatter and allure the multitude. At such a disadvan-
tage stands scientific truth against ecclesiasticism and
its gilded promissory. Yet there are many who see in
this aspect of nature and this wide free field for self-
development the earnest of loftier ideals, purer morals,
and a grander day for man.

Is it possible to save the soul?

There have been a great many theories of soul salvation. Every religious system treats of the problem —
usually by the summoning in of supernatural powers
and agencies, with rite and ritual. The point of chief
interest in all these promulgated systems of salvation,
the really significant point, is the evidence afforded of
the very strong hope and desire of humanity everywhere for prolonged life and immortality. With all
their vagaries the systems are so many evidences of
the strong desire of human beings for prolonged life.

Of how great avail these systems (embodying as they

always do the slowly developing ethics of the race)
have been for the encouragement and comfort of mankind through the darker, semi-brutal eras of race life,
it would be difficult to make a correct estimate; such
aid, indeed, can scarcely be over-estimated. And
although in the stronger, clearer light of later science,
the tenets of all olden creeds touching disembodied
soul life are seen to be invalidated, the hope of deathless life which found expression in them has been
fostered and transmitted from generation to generation.

Never stronger has been that desire and that hope of
immortality than to-day when the race, or at least the
civilized and educated branch of it, emerging from its
childhood into adolescence, casts myth and ditty away
and perceives the tale of disembodied souls to be a
fable of its infancy, a soothing tale to pacify its early
woes.

In this century we recognize for the first time our
real position as inhabitants of a globe in space. For
the first time the grandeur and the awe of our situation
presents itself as fact and truth, stripped of fable and
myth. The mighty opportunities, which the conquest
and control of the cosmic forces offer, begin to be perceived. Power, unlimited power lies idly pulsating in
semi-sentient macro-volts. Man has but to subjugate
and direct it, to be the architect of worlds, even, to
restore aged globes, to replenish the vast fires of failing
suns. There is neither let nor hindrance in cosmos.
No jealous deity tyrannizes; no malignant fiend thwarts.
We are alone. Alone on the grand illimitable. Solitary, but free. It is not very probable that the earth's
companion globes of this solar system are the *habitat*

of intelligent life.   What lives on or around other outer
suns, we know not; but within a radius of forty trillions of miles, we are beyond much doubt alone.   But
children no longer, we see ourselves alone and are not
afraid.   It is a glorious heritage of freedom.   We have
but to discover, invent, and rule all this cosmic pleni-
tude of empire.   To address prayers to the wide, little-
conscious *terraine* and sit passive to see them answered
in our behalf is idle.   The truer conception of universal beneficence makes us sure, too, that such shelter
would not be best.   We are the unaided free.   If we
want prolonged life, we must make shift to achieve it.
We shall die till we do achieve it; and were we to die
resignedly — as our philosophers would advise us —
resignedly forever, nature would still smile in eternal
calm.   Our fate and fortunes import not to *it*.   On the
other hand, we are under no obligation to *it*.   It is
ours to win, to hold, and to use.

The one element lacking to realize all this wealth of
freedom is *time*.   There is not time.   Before we have
fairly learned the rudiments of life, we suffer from disease and infirmity, and alas, must die, miserably die,
with all this infinite opportunity to live unentered, un-
enjoyed, unpossessed.   Death keeps humanity down to
a bootless learning and re-learning, over and over, of
the mere alphabet and accidence of life.   On account
of death the human generations scarcely more than hold
their own; for in dying the results of teaching are almost wholly lost; the succeeding generation scarcely
more than learns what its parents have learned.   Little
indeed of experience is really conserved; for the tissue
of intellect must mature for forty years to become really
wise.   Death causes all this vast labor to be done over

and over again, perhaps, on the whole, better, often
worse.   Reproduction is better than extinction, but
only a degree better, and not for a moment to be compared with the grand advantages of living on free from
personal death.

Reproduction takes place because we should otherwise die, but it is not an ideal mode of survival.   The
individual with his acquired experience and refinement
is the ideal survivor.   Infancy suffers what would be
needless tortures in learning to live, if the adult could
survive in health, with living matter fresh, growing, and
unshrunken.

The world-wide demand of educated, inventive man
is now for more time.   He sees the doctrine of disembodied souls to be a myth, and asks : *Is it possible
to save the soul?*   Salvation, in the old sacerdotal sense,
is the portrayal of an aspiration only ; but can we not
achieve prolonged life ?   The question is one that enters
with the newer conception of our freedom in the universe.   What we have we must achieve for ourselves.
We are alone here with everything to gain from invention, research, and discovery.

Immortality is the birthright of life and the destiny
of man.   Men still die, but death is not an irremediable
evil.   The great scheme of evolution of life, when
grasped in its entirety, points to a purified earth, inhabited by one great nationality, the decendants of mankind, whose lives will be prolonged toward immortality.
A *gens* terrestrial and celestial, not over peopling the
earth, nor yet devoid of procreative power ; not an as-
semblage of infirm, aged organisms, kept alive by improved medicaments ; but persons fresh in unfading

youth to whom aging will bring not infirmity, but
stronger personality, fuller life, grander beauty, and
greater wisdom.

The facts and the *rationale* of the preceding papers,
and of the inquiry as herein formulated, may be briefly
restated : —

In protoplasm, or the physico-vital state of matter,
in which alone terrestrial life exists, and from which
the evolution of life has taken place, there appears to
be the demonstration of a great truth of nature, namely,
that motion emanates outward from a sentient subjective
impulse deep at the heart, the core, of matter; that all
natural phenomena have a subjective source, primarily,
albeit there are many intermediate correlations of that
subjective impulse from out concentric estates of material
tenuity, ere what we first perceive as subjective takes
on the aspect of objective.

In a word, matter is not primarily *dead*, but subjective and sentient; and our proposition concerning it
makes to the effect that a lowly, primitive sentience
antedates movement, and is the primary cause of
motion; and that in protoplasm, this sentience assumes
the guidance of chemism and mechanical motion.
Sentience is the subjective side, or component, of universal matter; and matter when aggregated and combined in the protoplasmic state becomes living, that
is to say, self-actuating matter, by virtue of its sentient
property.

Such at least appears to be the more rational hypothesis of life, to wit, that it is correlated and identical
with that power or energy in nature of which we do

know something, rather than that it is a sporadic mani-
festation of a new and supposititious power of which
we know nothing.   For ultimately the question brings
us to this alternative.

Theoretically, matter, meaning ultimate matter,
might be defined as that remote, inner centre, or focus
of existence, whence our twin perceptions of energy
and of inertia emerge.   It is now probable that there
is no such thing as inert or lifeless matter; nor yet
any such condition of energy as pure force existing
apart from matter.   Were we bold enough to attempt
a definition of matter in a single word, that word would
be *Emanance.*

And why not Deity?

Because, it seems to me, that every right-minded
person must shrink from ascribing the "wide, sad
tragedy" of life, as enacted and suffered in its past and
even in its present course of evolution on the earth, to
the providence of an omnipotent, merciful, and all-wise
creator, believing such a conception to be immoral.
For it is only a purblind optimism that can see mercy,
wisdom, or justice throughout the long eras of injustice,
cruelty, and bloodshed of which earth has been the
theatre ever since life first stirred upon its surface.
We would ascribe the responsibility for it to no Being
who was able to prevent or alleviate it, but believe
rather that deity is an ideal of the human intellect, and
that it will be attained as a result of evolution on the
earth, in the apotheosis of man.

In protoplasm the living substance has slowly *felt* its
way, so as to speak, upward by organic steps, from
simple sentience to organized intelligence.   Sentience,
expressing itself in terms of life, has persisted, as if

from some inherent stress or impulse, to obtain, through organism, better and fuller development. That stress, that impulse, comes from the nascent perception of joy when sentience first stirs matter, in protoplasm. The lowliest polyp will make a grand struggle to save its life. Nature thus makes oath in every creature that life is indeed a boon and worth the living. In mankind the desire for extended life has grown into an aspiration for immortal life; and in all the great religious systems this aspiration has been projected forward as creed in the immortality of the soul. Immortal life in "heaven" has been "promised" as the incentive to and the reward for correct living. Immortal life, or, strictly speaking, more life, has been the ideal of the human era. "Salvation" from death and misery has been the dream of our race since very early times: the one bright hope never quite despaired of. But, like all the great instinctive aspirations of mankind, this one, in religious systems, has been adapted to man's condition of helplessness and weakness. The aspiration has been given a form of certainty to make it more effective.

At length, after centuries of dogma, erratic faith, and equally erratic doubt, we are in possession of facts from which a creed may be rationally forecast. Those facts demonstrate the continuous evolution of life under nature from lowliest forms to man: a long, weary, and unaided struggle upward through organization from the elemental sentience of matter to the human intellect. But is all this grand effort to terminate in the semi-brutal, half-developed creature, man, with all his ideals unrealized? Has evolution ceased? On the contrary, it is the writer's faith that we have as yet seen but the nether limb of evolution. Its grand complement has

still to be disclosed in the perfecting of the human
organism and the removal of the causes of disease, old-
aging and death ; in a word, the achievement of immortality.   Immortal life will be won by applied knowledge.
Man will save his own soul.   Earth is to be made
"heaven."   "Salvation" is to come from knowledge
and the apotheosis of the race.   This is what evolution
means.   This is what life on the earth is struggling
upward to win : Immortality, Happiness, Heaven ;
ideals to be realized by human effort.   The tenets of
all the great religious systems foreshadow it.   It is
time to understand this.   It is time to realize our true
situation on the earth, and cease from chasing mirage.
We have now sufficient knowledge to begin to save our
own souls.   As well face the facts of our mortal condition to-day as spend another thousand years doting
on fond illusions.   If we would live, we must save ourselves.   This is the religion of life ; the religion of self-
salvation.   It is not "atheism"; not "materialism," in
the old crass sense.   Not "infidelity"; rather Fidelity
to the best and the essential doctrines of all religions.
Not "scepticism," but Hope and Faith in Life.   Not the
"idle, new dream" of "Scientific Materialism," but the
Dream of all the Ages; the grand scheme of Nature,
maturing and going into effect since first our earth
became the theatre of life.

www.ingramcontent.com/pod-product-compliance
Lightning Source LLC
Chambersburg PA
CBHW030537270326
41927CB00008B/1415